Dear Claudia

I hope my book c

help you in your spiritual

toI growth.

Thank you for being such a great

Supporter of my work.

Lots of Love

Miki Jacobs

SOUL SECRETS

A Spiritual Guidebook for Contacting
Your "TEAM" - Spirit Guides, Angels,
and Departed Loved Ones

MIKI JACOBS

BALBOA
PRESS

A DIVISION OF HAY HOUSE

Balboa Press books may be ordered through booksellers or by contacting:

Balboa Press
A Division of Hay House
1663 Liberty Drive
Bloomington, IN 47403
www.balboapress.com
1 (877) 407-4847

Because of the dynamic nature of the Internet, any web addresses or
links contained in this book may have changed since publication and
may no longer be valid. The views expressed in this work are solely those
of the author and do not necessarily reflect the views of the publisher,
and the publisher hereby disclaims any responsibility for them.

The author of this book does not dispense medical advice or prescribe the use
of any technique as a form of treatment for physical, emotional, or medical
problems without the advice of a physician, either directly or indirectly. The
intent of the author is only to offer information of a general nature to help you
in your quest for emotional and spiritual well-being. In the event you use any
of the information in this book for yourself, which is your constitutional right,
the author and the publisher assume no responsibility for your actions.

Any people depicted in stock imagery provided by Thinkstock are models,
and such images are being used for illustrative purposes only.
Certain stock imagery © Thinkstock.

Printed in the United States of America.

ISBN: 978-1-4525-2369-9 (sc)
ISBN: 978-1-4525-2370-5 (e)

Balboa Press rev. date: 10/30/2014

CONTENTS

DEDICATION

This book is dedicated to my beloved husband Clayton for his great support of my work and immense love in my life. Also to my TEAM in spirit; the Archangel Michael, my Guardian Angels: Iris and Judah, and my Spirit Guides: Barmenada and Lochem, as well as the Archangels Gabriel, Raphael, and Uriel, for all of their love, support, and guidance in my life and assistance in writing this book.

INTRODUCTION

I was not "born" a medium. Arriving to my spiritual path and to my ability to communicate with spirits started later in life, when I was in my early thirties. Prior to that, as an Israeli Jewish woman I followed and practiced Judaism. However, at one point some of my religious rules and beliefs did not reflect who I was anymore or how I viewed both my life and the world around me. It was then that I decided to change from religion to spirituality.

It was in the course of my spiritual path and later on through my ability to communicate with spirits that I discovered the concept of the "Team". In my work when I use the word Team I refer to a group of spirits that accompanies each one of us from birth to death. Our Team members include our Spirit Guides, Guardian Angels, Archangels, departed loved ones, and sometimes the Elementals, or Nature Spirits. The purpose of our Team in general is to guide, support, protect, and help us use life on this planet for the sake of our soul's growth and evolution.

Over the years I have realized that the way I discovered my spiritual path as well as my self-taught channeling is important for people to hear because a common belief is that one is either born with mediumship abilities or not which, of course, from my own experience was not the case. A big part of my work as a medium and as a spiritual teacher, whether it is through private readings and consultations, groups readings, or workshops and lectures for people around the world, includes teaching people how they can do it too, assuming of course, that they are willing to do the necessary daily spiritual work and are interested in communicating with spirits. My work also includes connecting people to their Team in the Spirit World as well as connecting people to their departed loved ones.

In this book I share with you in great detail the concept of the Team. I describe each Team member, their unique purpose in our life, and the various ways in which they communicate with us and why they do so. In this book I also describe how I got to know my own Team and how specifically I taught myself to communicate with each one of them. Although this book is mainly about the Team concept, because I wanted to include some additional spiritual teaching, I also share with you information that I have gathered over the years from channeling spirits regarding other spiritual topics that I know are very important for you to understand and learn about. I divided this book into two parts. The first part includes all theconcepts and the information that you will need to have as afoundation for the second part of the book which is the practicalpart where you will use the tools and practice the concepts in yourdaily life.

I hope that you find the way I wrote this book to be simple and easy to understand. Not only because I did not have much of a choice since English is my second language and so I could not use too many fancy words, but more importantly because as a teacher I believe that simplicity is crucial for teaching spirituality so that all people, those who are already spiritually aware and, more so, those new to their spiritual path, can more easily understand the information, concepts, and tools and apply them to their life.

I hope that this book helps you get to know your Team members and communicate with them so that you will KNOW without a doubt how loved and cared for you are and that you are NEVER alone. I also hope that the information in my book about other spiritual subtopics will help you to grow in awareness, become a better more spiritual human being, and help you create a heaven on Earth kind of a life.

PART ONE

Theory – Understanding The Concepts

In this theory part of the book I will provide you with valuable information that will help you clear a path for your connection to your Team members and your ability to communicate with them. In this section of the book I will also cover various important spiritual topics that are both necessary and helpful for your spiritual growth in general and for your connection to your Team specifically.

CHAPTER ONE

Our Incarnations On Earth

Incarnation is the base concept of all spiritual studies and spiritual growth which is why I will introduce it here in my first chapter.

It is my belief that any kind of spiritual information or spiritual teaching will not make sense without fully understanding first why we are on this harsh planet. I will describe the concept of incarnation with the hope that it will help you to better understand the information about our "Team" in the Spirit World as well as to lay a foundation for the other spiritual topics and subjects that I cover later in this book.

Throughout many lifetimes, our soul is always in a state of growth toward a higher level of consciousness. The more spiritually aware the soul is, the more the Creator's characteristics are able to be expressed. Every soul has its own preference for ways of advancing its evolution and every soul grows at its own pace. Some souls work on their awareness in the Spirit World, while others choose to experience life on other planets with different forms of realities.

However, for an accelerated growth, all souls will sooner or later choose to incarnate into the most effective school-like planet of all, Earth. This is where we find ourselves now. In an Earthly incarnation our soul divides its overall energy and leaves the majority of its energy behind in the Spirit World. Using a small portion of this energy, it enters a physical body and experiences life as a human being. The energy that resides in the body is sometimes referred to as the "Higher Self".

Due to the harsh nature of life on Earth, the many limitations of the human body, and the complexity of a human being's mind, incarnating into a human form presents our soul an opportunity to experience life in a foreign dimension. One that is completely different than our true home, the timeless and boundless reality of the Spirit World.

These unique conditions that planet Earth has to offer create for our souls an unlimited amount of opportunity for accelerated growth. Being "stuck" in the dense physical body for many years at a time, a journey on Earth is an extremely draining experience for our soul. At the end of each life, all human souls must "clear up" our energy field from any negative residue collected from the life we just lived in order to become whole again, refreshed, and to eventually experience yet another incarnation.

During an Earthly incarnation there are two main ways in which our soul grows and advances its evolution. One is through the process of enlightenment and the other is through activating the universal law of karma. Enlightenment happens when we are able to de-identify from our Ego, the negative part of our mind/personality, in order to allow our Higher Self to govern our life and express to the world the beautiful characteristics that we inherited from the Creator. Karma, the law of "pay-back", is when our soul grows through using life consequences to clear and balance any negativity that the personality has accumulated in current or previous incarnations.

Incarnation is our soul's choice. Our soul decides when to incarnate, into what kind of a life circumstances, and what it must accomplish in each lifetime in order to advance its spiritual awareness. No one forces or urges us to enter a physical body or to repeat life again. It is important to mention here that the Creator, while having designed the beautiful concept of incarnation and indeed aware of our soul's evolution and growth, is not involved in any way with the planning of our incarnations nor with its timing or outcomes. The Creator allows us to be and allows us to grow in any way we choose to.

In any given incarnation, major events and significant people that we will share our life with are all pre-designed by our soul prior to entering a body. The details of an Earthly incarnation are referred to as the life's "blueprint".

The pre-designed "blueprint" of an incarnation includes the physical and mental bodies, the number of years that we are going to occupy the body, and when and how we are going to exit it, meaning when and how we are going to die. Our soul also carefully chooses the precise moment when we are born, in what part of the world, into what country, our race, gender, childhood conditions, parents, siblings, significant close friends, and life partners, just to name a few of the infinite pre-conditions that are worked out in advance. Major events that occur during our incarnation such as illness, marriage, divorce, or any major loss, are also a part of our soul's pre-designed plan. I understand that sometimes it is difficult to accept that it was our soul who chose the life we are now living, especially if our daily life is consumed with worries, problems and challenges, and whose life isn't? It is also understandable that when life is difficult, the last thing we want to hear is that the difficulties we encounter and endure are pre-designed, and therefore are actually planned and necessary for our soul's growth. It seems incomprehensible that our soul would freely choose to leave the serene and beautiful Spirit World and incarnate over and over again into this harsh planet where suffering and pain are an inevitable part of life.

However, as with many spiritual concepts, it is very important to remember that I am presenting here the perspective of our soul and not the mind. You, the person reading this chapter, and me, the one writing it, belong to a species that is governed by the mind. Because our mind is only concerned with, and relies solely on the five senses to interpret reality, it believes only in what it can see, hear, smell, touch, or taste. The mind knows nothing of the incarnation, nor of our soul, the wise and powerful entity that carefully planned it. In life, our mind makes us believe that it is solely up to us to "make it or break it" and that any experiences, outcomes, or challenges, can be avoided or resolved with better luck, better thinking, or more effective planning. Sometimes of course, to some extent, this is true. However, what the mind does not understand and often refuses to accept is that the majority of our experiences in life are there for one main reason: to serve our soul's growth!

If we follow the scenario created by the mind, that nothing in life is pre-designed and that we are the only ones who can control all our life events and outcomes, both the good and the bad ones, why then is it that sometimes things just simply cannot be fixed, resolved, or changed despite the hard work, good planning, or better thinking? Why is it that sometimes the mind can not possibly explain nor understand certain events, outcomes, and situations, especially ones that do not make any sense such as a sudden illness, unexplained "accident", an unexpected loss, death of a baby or young child, or the fact that some of the "good people" in this world die young while the "bad people" live a long life? If we were to leave the planning of an incarnation to our mind it would choose a life where there is never any need for any spiritual work, or any work at all for that matter. Our mind would clearly plan a life where we would be born into the perfect loving nurturing family, we would never have to worry about money, always find jobs that are pleasant and fulfilling, we would find our perfect soul mate and live happily ever after, stay healthy, have the perfect body shape, eat all we want and never gain a pound (my favorite), live until we are ninety years old, and then, ever so peacefully, die in our sleep without any suffering. Sounds good? Not from the perspective of our soul. Remember that our soul knows planet Earth for what it is: a temporary spiritual school that provides an unlimited amount of growth opportunities. And so, difficult, painful, and fearful experiences, are considered to be effective ways of speeding up the growth process and will always be included in any given incarnation's "blueprint". An illness in an incarnation, for example, presents for our soul the ultimate opportunity for rapid growth as well as an opportunity for balancing any karmic debt. Through an illness, a person can learn the power of faith, trust, patience, acceptance, surrender, empathy, and compassion. Traits that will add to the soul's overall awareness. Of course, the concept of sickness being a "good thing" is easier to accept when we are healthy and not ill. Sometimes during the course of my work, when I come across gravely ill people and explain to them the nature of their illness from the perspective of their soul's journey, their initial reaction is naturally anger or denial. "How can my cancer be something that my soul chose?" However, if the person is somewhat spiritually inclined, the spiritual explanation for their illness will eventually provide a kind of comfort against the negative and destructive explanations that their mind has to offer such as; "God is punishing me", I suffer because I am a bad person","I am just unlucky, poor me". And the mind's favorite destructive phrase of all: "Why me?". It is important to understand that in an incarnation there is no bad luck, being doomed, punished, or being a bad person. There are only opportunities for growth. The next time someone tells you that "Things happen for a reason" do not discount that phrase as a "wishy-washy" cliché, but rather as a true and wise spiritual concept. Authentically understanding that from the perspective of our soul, that things in life do happen for a reason will provide you with a great deal of comfort, especially if you are going through difficult, unpleasant, or seemingly unbearable experiences.

In our Earthly incarnations, we all have an up and down path through life. No one, ever, has a life that is always bad or always good. From the perspective of our immortal and fearless soul, an "up and down" kind of a life, where certain aspects of life are fairly stable and calm, while others are challenging and difficult, is much more effective for growth than a "flatlined" life, where things don't change and always stay the same. Besides, in order to appreciate and enjoy the "up" times in life, we must first experience and learn from the "down" times.

Another major contributing factor to our soul's growth during an Earthly incarnation and in the Spirit World is free will. Free will is a universal law that must be fully honored and respected among us human beings on Earth and among all souls/beings in the Spirit World. No one is allowed to impose or interfere with our free will, not our Team, other spirits, Angels, and not even the Creator. Free will allows us the freedom to choose right from wrong and then learn and grow from the consequences of our choices. It allows each one of us to grow in our own way and at our own pace. Free will is the Creator's gift to us and the ultimate, unconditional, expression of love for us. Throughout our lives on Earth, choices and decisions that we make using our free will, ultimately determine the incarnation's successes and failures. Also, free will can greatly influence the blueprint of an upcoming incarnation. So the good news is that free will gives us the freedom of choice, and allows us to do what we want to do. The bad news is that this freedom must be executed carefully. If we are reckless or unwise with the way we exercise our free will, we can negatively affect our life and other people's lives, in this incarnation, the afterlife, and future incarnations. So carefully observe your choices and decisions and avoid foolish, destructive, and reckless acts, in order to give your journey the opportunity to unfold the way it should and for as long as it was meant to. Do not act in ways that might cause your life to take the wrong path. Avoid choices that originate from the Ego. Use the choices that are governed by your Higher Self. Ego-based choices can be recognized because they usually lack any consideration for oneself or for others. They are hasty, impatient, arrogant, selfish, and may even be dangerous. They are choices that will affect your well- being, distort your life path, and delay or block any spiritual growth. If a person chooses to drink and drive for example, which is a classic selfish and reckless choice, they risk killing themselves, or worse, someone else. With this irresponsible decision, they might cut their own life short, or the life of another person prematurely, when otherwise the Earthly journey was supposed to continue. Drunk driving might also injure the people involved mentally and emotionally, which could scar them for life, and thus prevent their pre-designed journey from unfolding the way it was meant to. The bottom line is that although the precise time of death is predetermined by our soul prior to entering the body, and despite the great amount of protection that we are provided with on Earth, true accidents can and will occur. If we act stupidly, we will get hurt, harm, kill someone else, or die! The unfortunate outcome of the extreme example of drinking and driving can be applied to any other reckless and irresponsible choices that we might make. Of course, the more reckless the choice, the more severe the consequences and a wrong choice, will always remain a wrong choice. Someone, in one way or another, and to one extreme or another, will get hurt.

In any given incarnation, the degree of a person's spiritual awareness can greatly affect the way that they use their free will. The more spiritually aware a person becomes, the less likely they will be to misuse their free will with Ego-based, negative, and reckless choices or actions, and more likely to use it for choices and actions that are fair, carefully considered, positive in nature, are based on honesty, loyalty, acceptance, compassion, and most of all, on love.

Appreciate, value, and guard your life! Not just because you do not want to die and leave this planet and the people that you love, but more importantly, because your soul invested a great deal of time and effort planning this incarnation and this life, for your soul's growth. Fully accepting that your life on Earth is a crucial part of your overall soul's evolution will help you to understand that all your experiences, the good and joyful ones, the difficult and unpleasant ones, as well as all the significant relationships, especially the difficult ones, in the past, present, and future, are meant to bring up to the surface what you need to learn, and must work on in order to contribute to your soul's spiritual growth.

> **Do not waste your life! For as long as you are here on this planet, be wise, be brave, be courageous, and be loving, because your soul needs and relies on you to successfully complete this incarnation so that it can move forward with its evolutionary process.**

CHAPTER TWO

Discovering My Spiritual Path

I did not arrive at my spiritual path until later in life, when I was in my early thirties, and, unlike most mediums who inherently knew about their abilities to see, hear, and communicate with the Spirit World from a very young age, I did not see, hear, or sense anything that resembled a spirit until later in life.

In this chapter I will share with you how I transitioned myself to spirituality. I will also describe the way I taught myself how to meditate, channel spirits, and finally begin the spiritual work I do today as a medium.

From Religion To Spirituality

I was born and raised in Israel and grew up in a traditional and somewhat orthodox Jewish home. At the age of eighteen, like all people in my country, I served in the Israeli army for three years.

After the army, I traveled around the world and came to reside in California where I found the weather and style of people to be similar to that of my native country. I have lived here ever since. In 1987 with a partner and then husband, Richard, we opened our own glazing company, an automotive and commercial glass company in Long Beach, California, which we ran for eighteen years.

In the first few years, after arriving to the United States, I continued to practice the Jewish traditions and customs of my religion and I must say, that at that time, I was as far from spirituality as one could possibly be. Fighting for the Israeli army had led me to believe that war between countries could bring peace. I was afraid of a mean, harsh God, and certainly did not believe much about life after death, spirits, or Angels. Living in the United States, however, three thousand miles away from my native country of Israel, I was exposed to many other different religions and to spirituality, which encouraged me to dig deeper and reevaluate the validity of some of my religious beliefs and concepts. With that evaluation process, I came to the realization that continuing to follow some of the practices of Judaism did not quite reflect who I was or what I thought of myself, my life, other people, our planet, or God. In fact, the more I studied about religions in general, the more I became convinced that religions in our world were more of a separator among people than the connectors and the unifiers that they claimed to be. I also concluded that in many aspects, the religions of the world were more about power and control and were less about love. Since there is almost always some goodness in things, and although some aspects of most religions I believe are indeed fake and negative, some aspects are positive and loving; it is up to us to be aware of both. Here is an example of this. If you go to church on Sunday, or to a synagogue on Saturday, in order to pray and express your authentic love and gratitude for the Creator, that is wonderful and positive. However, if you listen to and believe someone describing to you a conditional God that loves some people, and not others, that is plain wrong. Or, if your religion has a set of rules that instruct you to judge other people that do not follow the same set of beliefs that you do, that is also negative and wrong. Even the love-based beliefs of a religion must be authentically followed. For example, sharing love with other people every Sunday in church is lovely. Acting in an unkind and judgmental manner to others the rest of the week is frankly an insult to the Creator. You may as well stay home. I have learned that the rule of thumb when engaging with any religion is to follow love, a pure, authentic, unconditional love, that includes everyone. Stay away from rigid rules and from a fake love that is conditional or judgmental. Most of all, no matter what religion you follow, stay away from any group who claims that God is exclusively theirs.

As I continued to re-evaluate my own, as well as other religious beliefs, I found myself with many questions that were not being answered. For example, I often wondered about the validity of the Jewish nation of Israel claiming to be "God's chosen people" and yet maintaining God's unconditional love to all people and all religions. That paradox certainly did not make sense to me as one claim was not congruent with the other. Other concepts, held by other religions, did not make sense to me either. I could not understand how anyone could claim to kill "in the name of God", and then, having committed the killings, claim that God's promise to them is an eternal life in Heaven. That a God that instructs them to kill innocent people and children just because they have a different set of beliefs is also the God that they claim to be such a loving and peace seeking entity. This is ridiculous, obviously! At that point, as I broadened my studies about religions and more clearly formulated my opinion about them, I felt that I was gradually detaching myself from most of the concepts and rules of my own religion. I decided to become pickier about my beliefs, and more selective in what I would follow. Of course, I was still proud of being an Israeli woman, still proud of my Jewish heritage which is why I decided to continue and follow the good aspects of Judaism: the love-base beliefs, and leave the bad beliefs behind which were the rules and regulations that made no sense to me any longer, and that were obviously written by human beings' Egos. It was then that I felt that spirituality might be the path for me and switched from my religious studies to spiritual studies. I expanded my spiritual knowledge and learned about different cultures and their spiritual perspectives on life, life after death, the Spirit World, planet Earth, and other planets. Also, a large part of my spiritual studies at the time was learning about the Creator.

The Creator That I Found

When I was growing up, I remember the vision I had of God: a bearded male figure with a cane, somewhat like Moses. I also imagined this God to be harsh, judgmental, and even scary. I was convinced that he was always watching over every move I made and every step I took, looking down at me and examining me carefully to see if I was following his rules (which of course were different than other religions' rules). To a lesser degree, the childhood beliefs I had of God, continued into my adult life. However, as I became more and more detached from my religion and making the shift into spirituality, I wanted to discover a different God than the one I grew up with. I wanted to get to know that powerful and wise, yet soft and loving Creator that I intuitively felt connected to and unconditionally loved by. Next, I will share with you my current views and beliefs about the spiritual Creator that I have found through my spiritual path.

God is energy... vast, boundless, and eternal. This force is the source of all creation, and therefore is a part of creation itself, including human beings, spirit beings, animals, nature, planet Earth, other planets, galaxies, and whole universes. The essence of this energy is pure divine love and can never have any negative characteristics. This means that the energy of God can not judge us, punish us, love

14

one person and not another, kill one person at an early age while giving another person a long life, cause children to die, or prefer one race over another. Nor does he care if we follow a certain religion, pray to him or not, or even whether we believe in his existence at all. God holds a complete and utter unconditional love for all of us. This kind of divine love is the kind that we human beings are incapable of comprehending on Earth. This divine love is a completely different kind of love than the one that we feel toward ourselves, other human beings, our partners, siblings, parents, or even our children. It is the kind of love that cannot be experienced with the limitation of the physical mind. The concept of the Creator being an energy force that can only hold a pure unconditional love for us will help you better understand that you are not bound by some "man-made" contrived rules and regulations that must be followed in order to "earn" his love. It will free you from any cultural or religious beliefs about the kind of God that you need to please. God is very much aware of our daily lives on Earth. Although he knows of our struggles, successes, weaknesses, and strengths, he is not directly involved with our day-to-day affairs. I understand that this concept will be difficult for some of you to accept. The common belief that most people hold is that in life, when we are happy, successful, healthy, peaceful, struggling, ill, or poor, it is God that directly influences those experiences and outcomes. We believe that he can "give us things", and then, just like that, can take them away from us. We believe that God has an active hand in each experience we have on Earth. That concept is wrong. Not being involved in our lives does not mean that God is careless about us or our well-being. Nor does it means that he is not aware of the progress that we are making in our overall soul evolution as individuals, as well as the human race as a whole. He loves us, cares for us, and is proud of us. As I stated before, everyone and everything is a part of God's energy. However, by not interfering, judging, or influencing our decisions and actions, God gives us the freedom to express ourselves uniquely in order to successfully accomplish our journey. He allow us to grow in our own ways and at our own pace. He exhibits toward us the ultimate unconditional divine love. If God were to interfere with our lives on our level, we would be reduced to machine-like or robotic beings, walking around without the ability to choose and create on our own.

Although not directly involved in our affairs, God has created certain universal laws and "programs", as I like to refer to them, that are put into place in order for his creation to continue and function in an orderly, fair, and organized manner. The Angelic Kingdom, the Spirit World, the Nature Kingdom, as well as Planet Earth each have its own unique sets of universal laws and programs for all of the participants in these realities to obey and follow. Our planet, the physical realm, has its own unique set of laws and programs. Examples of these programs are free will, karma and reincarnation. These are only some of the necessary universal laws and programs that we, human beings, must follow. They are specifically designed to create the perfect "school-like" environment for our souls while in the physical body. That means that the universal law of free will allows us the freedom to choose a path or action and then use the experiences that we have created by our choice for spiritual growth. Karma for example is the law of "pay-back". This is where every one of us, without exception, must be held accountable for our own actions and then experience the consequences accordingly. Incarnation is the program that gives our soul the opportunity to re-enter another body, over and over again, in order to experience life from many different perspectives and conditions in the physical realm and use them for growth.

The mere mental belief that God exists is not enough. It is not enough to pray to him, praise him with spoken words, or read books about him. Believing in God, requires spiritual work, especially in our Earthly lives where our doubtful mind tends to be a creature of habit and remain stuck with certain cultural beliefs, or refuses to accept anything that is not validated by the five sense reality. A true spiritual belief means that you understand that your soul, the energy that resides in the body, is what represents God on planet Earth since we are a spark of his energy. That means that you need to accept God as an energetic force, then learn the characteristics and nature of this force, and then finally, express these characteristics that you have incorporated into your daily life as well as out into this world. In essence, we need to be like God. Not in an Ego sense of the word, but in the spiritual sense of it. For example, you need to acknowledge God's equal unconditional love to all life forms without exception. This means that although a human being expresses the Creator's energy differently from an animal, and an animal expresses this energy differently than a tree or a rock, they are all equally valued and cherished by him as they all have their own unique purpose in the overall creation. And so you, like God, must live life with the intention of authentically cherishing and loving all of his creation. On the other hand, when we hate, judge, envy others, or believe that animals are less-valued life forms than human beings and deserve less respect, or when we take our beautiful planet for granted and, consequently, are careless in its preservation you side with the judgmental negative nature of your personality and you drift away from the loving nature of your soul and, therefore, away from God. Stay connected to the Creator by observing and acknowledging his creation and then hold gratitude that you are an inseparable part of it. How do you do this? Use your gifts of imagination and observation. These tools were built into you for this very purpose. Attempt to see and feel the Creator everywhere. Look up at the stars in a clear night and observe the vastness and the beauty of that endless space. Think how amazing and powerful that force must be, to have created the planets, stars, and galaxies. The ones that we are able to see to the countless ones that we can not. Take the time to go out and enjoy the beauty of nature. Observe the fractal nature of God in the forms that nature takes. See how everything operates in such an amazing and endless complexity. How all creatures, flowers and trees are lovingly being provided for, and are taken care of in the magical natural order, without human control or intervention. Be present at sunrise and sunset, and feel yourself merge with the beauty and power of these daily miracles. Learn about the human physical body, the brain, the nervous system, the immune system, the divisions of the cells, the various organs, the actual miracle in the creation of new life, and the amazing process of birth. Then, acknowledge the indescribable wisdom of God that was able to create such an incredible "mechanism". A machine that has its own divine intelligence and its own defense mechanisms in order to protect and sustain itself. Perhaps the most important thing to do to connect the physical body to the spiritual energy, is to make a habit of paying attention to your breathing. This involuntary, automatic function, is what keeps us alive and keeps us connected to the rest of the living creatures as well as to the Source. This miracle, that we often take for granted, is not only a system of symbiotic connection of inhaling oxygen provided by the vegetative world and exhaling carbon dioxide that in turn supplies them with life, but is also the way that we energize our body and soul with God's ineffable Chi energy. It is through this miraculous exchange of energy that occurs every moment of our lives that is the most basic way to connect with God and every aspect of his creation.

My Self-Taught Channeling

In this section, I will share with you how I taught myself to communicate with spirits. Here, when I talk about meditation and automatic writing, I will describe it in a very general way. However, in the practical section of this book, when I will be teaching you how to communicate with your Team, I will provide you with explanations of much greater detail and depth.

Over the years, while operating my day-time business in addition to my spiritual education and studies I had a strong, nagging, intuitive feeling that I needed to learn about meditation. I researched all kinds of meditation. I learned about the different purposes of meditation as well as the different cultures and their individual and unique meditation techniques. Then, once I felt that I was well informed about the spiritual concepts of meditation and techniques, I started to practice it myself. My first task was to work on my ability to quiet my mind and to get to the point where my mind was no longer active while I meditated. No longer thinking or worrying about my life, my past, my future, or about what was for breakfast at the end of the session. I recall putting meditation as a top priority in my life. I meditated every day except Sundays. Almost nothing came before my mediation sessions. I made a promise to myself to never skip a session. I was determined to succeed and determined to keep that promise. It was my intuition about the importance of meditation that kept pushing me forward, urging me not to stop, and was very helpful to me especially on days that I felt lazy, tired, or simply fed up with the whole thing. The good news was that I started to realized that the more I meditated the easier it was for me to quiet my mind and, more importantly, I noticed that once my mind was quiet I was able to enter a completely different state of being. In that state I felt as if I was not myself anymore, so to speak. I felt serene and calm. I felt as if time had stopped. In fact, that feeling was timeless. And in the midst of that wonderful feeling I also felt that all my life challenges, circumstances, and experiences, as well as all the people that I shared my life with and loved so dearly were of no concern at that moment. Not in a cold or negative way, but rather in a detached and distanced sort of a feeling. As if this were *my* life, *my* journey, and they had *their* own. I often refer to that feeling as being neutral and it is an absolutely fantastic feeling! I remember that once I got into this state of being, I did not want to lose that feeling and was actually afraid to stop meditating in case my ability to get there would diminish. And so, naturally, I just kept on going. I continued to practice meditation for over a year until I knew that I had mastered the process. It was then that I decided that it was the time for me to "lift it up a notch" and try to use my meditation to connect to the Spirit World. The question then became, how was I going to do that? Up until that point, in my spiritual path, channeling was something that I read about and was familiar with, but certainly nothing that I had experienced for myself and had always thought that the ability to connect to spirits was something that you must be born with. I was not aware of having ever sensed, heard, or seen a spirit up until that time, and I certainly could not have predicted anything. However, that helpful "nagging feeling", that intuitive guidance, kept urging me once again to try it anyway. And I did. One morning, I started my mediation session in the usual way; however this time I got a notebook and a pen and decided to ask spirit a question and write down what I heard, if anything. In essence I used a simple form of automatic writing, although back then I did not refer to it by that name. I said "If there are any spirits around, or any family member that has crossed over that wishes to talk to me, please do so, show me a sign!", I also asked for advice on a specific decision about my life and any information that I might need. I got nothing. I went home and tried again the next morning, and the next one. Weeks and then months went by with nothing. Every morning, same question, same anticipation, same results. I did, however, write down my own feelings of frustration about the process. It went something like this, "I am sitting here, and hearing nothing... I am not sure if I am doing it wrong, or perhaps there is no one around me... I wonder if there are no such things as spirits or Angels, or Spirit World... I wonder if I was wrong. Perhaps we *are* alone!". It was as if I were documenting me talking to myself and describing my feelings about it. It was certainly more like a journal rather than an automatic writing. I remember how silly I often felt, to be talking to myself, complaining and answering my own questions, one morning after another. I was feeling as though I was getting into an unproductive and frustrating cycle that had no meaningful results. At the time, each morning, staying in bed felt like a much better option than going outside and trying the same thing over and over again. I was ready to give up. Yet, each time I was ready to skip a session, my nagging dedication kicked in and I continued on. And then one morning something changed, *finally!* Why that morning the change happened, I do not know, other than to assume that spirits were finally able to get through to me, energetically speaking. Obviously they knew that I was ready. On that particular morning, in my morning meditation I heard a voice and the voice said, "I love you". Although the voice came from within me, *like* my inner voice, it was still very obvious that it wasn't my inner voice. It "felt" different. The new voice was softer and loving. It felt as if someone else were talking to me, not me talking to myself. There was an undeniable difference. It sounded nothing like my own inner voice, the voice I was accustomed to hearing for thirty-plus years. I also remember that the voice continued talking to me even when my conscious mind was thinking and when my usual inner voice was active. It was as if simultaneously I had two separate voices within my head, one in front, so to speak, and the other in the background. Needless to say, how excited I felt that morning and how surprised I was to experience such a weird sensation of an extra voice in my head! I could not believe that I had made contact with the Spirit World. I was so proud of myself for not giving up. I was thankful that my hard work and dedication finally produced a result. I was mostly grateful for that inner guidance, that "gut feeling", that always pushed me to continue onward with my spiritual path. I was grateful to my Soul. The next day I practically ran outside to start my meditation, anxious to discover if that voice would talk to me again. And sure enough, it was there again. This time I asked, "Who are you?" and the answer was, *"It is me, the Archangel Michael."* I almost fell off of my chair.

During the time when I started my channeling, I experienced many fearful thoughts and doubts. I was afraid that I might have a mental illness, such as schizophrenia that caused me to have this second voice in my head. I constantly doubted that it was indeed an Angel that was speaking to me, I often told myself, "It can not possibly be..." However, that beautiful loving voice that sounded so clear and felt so real continued to ease my fears and continued to validate its identity that it was indeed him, the Archangel Michael, speaking to me. Over time, I gradually gave up my fears and doubts and gratefully accepted this blessing. From then on, every morning while meditating I would connect with the Archangel Michael and hear his loving voice expressing supporting and loving phrases to me like, "I am always with you, you are safe, you are never alone!" And my favorite, "Do not be fearful!" It is difficult to describe the joyful feeling I have while communicating with the Archangel Michael. It was an absolutely amazing feeling and almost addictive. Every single time that the Archangel Michael spoke, I had tears of joy in my eyes, I had goosebumps, and an overwhelming feeling of being loved, protected, and cared for. As time went by, my conversations with Archangel Michael become deeper and more meaningful. No longer just half-sentences and scattered words but more complex messages with real and fascinating information. For the following months I continued to channel the Archangel Michael. He was always so very loving and always came forward with information about anything and everything that I wanted to know on every topic and subject. He spoke about himself, other Angels, the Angelic Kingdom, Nature Kingdom and other planets, aliens, UFOs, planet Earth, and about the Creator. The Archangel Michael also helped me with my own life as I often asked him for advice about decisions that I needed to make, and welcomed his guidance and support about challenges that I needed to face. He was helping me to be strong and fearless, to become a better human being. He was my invisible friend that helped change my life forever. One day, I heard a second voice in my head that introduced himself to me. He said that his name was *"Barmenanda"* and that he was my Spirit Guide, my teacher in the Spirit World. Later, I decided to nickname him "B". B's words were also loving, supportive, reassuring and encouraging. He, too, described who he was, his relationship to me and his role in my life, his many incarnations on Earth and about his many life experiences. Like the Archangel Michael, B was forthcoming with any information that I wanted to know or wished to learn about. And although as informative as Archangel Michael was, I realized that his messages were different. Archangel Michael spoke more about broad topics such as other universes, galaxies, and the Spirit World. In contrast, B's messages were more practical and more focused on physical life here on Earth, about the human being's Ego, and other day-to-day topics that humanity is now facing. He spoke, for example, about the influence of money on our lives, about illness, relationships, and dying and death. He, too, often advised me about my own life, mostly focusing on my Ego's weaknesses, and on the various ways that I could learn to discipline it. B is a true teacher: kind, loving, and patient, yet tough when its needed. I feel such an immense love toward this beautiful teacher of mine. I am so grateful for his wisdom and so blessed by his company. To this point, I had channeled Archangel Michael and Barmenanda when, one day, a third voice appeared in my head. By that time I was neither surprised nor confused and, for some reason, had actually anticipated another spirit joining in. When the third voice spoke with me, I sensed that his energy, his style of teaching, and type of messages were more similar to those of B than to those of the Archangel Michael's. Through this "knowing" I recognized him to be my second Spirit Guide, which later he confirmed. This time, however, getting my new Spirit Guide's name was not an easy task. For some reason I could not channel his name clearly and certainly could not pronounce it. His name sounded so weird, unusual, and unlike any name that we would hear on our planet. I remember expressing to him my great disappointment and frustration with not being able to understand his name and his loving reply to me was, "Then invent a name for me", which I did. I named him "*Lochem*",which in Hebrew translates to warrior, and he certainly is. A short time later, two new unfamiliar voices appeared and when I asked for their identity was told that they were my Guardian Angels. They told me that their names were "Iris" and "Judah". These two beautiful Angels have child-like, light, uplifting, and happy energies. Each time I channel them my body is filled with immense joy and serenity. They, too, explained who they were, why they were with me, and their role in my life on Earth. Over time, as I became more acquainted with my Guardian Angels, I realized that their messages were mainly concerned with my physical, mental, and emotional well-being. These two beloved Light Beings always help me to feel safe and secure by reassuring me that they are always by my side, protecting me, and that I am safe. What a wonderful feeling to know how protected I am. I specifically feel their protection in the car while driving. I suspect it is because they know that I am a somewhat nervous driver and they are more attentive to me when I drive. Now I have these four beautiful spirits to accompany me. Every day I connect to them and channel information, sometimes about my life and sometimes about any other topic or subject that I am interested in. Often, I simply meditate quietly and enjoy their company and their amazing, soothing, energy. We are a happy little group. One day, I expressed how grateful I was for their constant help with my spiritual growth. Their answer to me was that when I grew they grew as well. They said that they needed me as much as I needed them and that we were all a part of a "Team"! They continued to explain that growing was never one-sided, and when souls interact with one another, whether they were on planet Earth, the Spirit World, or other worlds, through these interactions there was always an exchange of energy that was beneficial for everyone's growth and evolution. It was then that my *Team* also explained to me that all people on planet Earth were also part of their own unique *Teams,* and that the *Team* concept played a crucial role in our Earthly incarnations.

The Beginning of My Mediumship Work

In 2005, a major event happened that changed the direction of my spiritual path and my soul's journey on Earth. Richard, my business partner of eighteen years, suddenly and tragically passed away at the age of forty-two. With his passing, the energy that kept our business together collapsed and our business closed its doors. That was a frightening time in my life. With English as my second language, a very strong accent that was difficult to understand, and only having a high school education, it was difficult for me to find an employer that would be willing to hire me. I was worried and uncertain about the future of my professional life. It was then that I was inspired by my Spirit Guides to use my channeling to help other people and to become a professional medium. I must admit, at first, I was very skeptical of this idea. I was overwhelmed by the thought of all the hard work that I would need to invest in creating a new business, especially a business so different from the one I owned and operated for so many years. I also knew that over the years, although I continuously channeled the Spirit World, up until then I had only channeled for myself and people that I knew such as close friends and family. The idea of channeling for "real" clients made me nervous. Again, however, I had a strong "knowingness", a gut feeling, that I could do it and would be great at it. I was actually able to foresee and sense the joy that this spiritual work would bring to me. It was as if despite all the questions and self doubts, this line of work was calling my name. It was at that time, that I also clearly realized that all of my life experiences up until that moment, all my spiritual studies, my fascination with the Spirit World, my meditation, my channeling, and even the unfortunate failure of my business, all contributed to the direction that I was about to take. Everything made sense and felt as if all the pieces of my life's puzzle perfectly fell into place! And so with the encouragement of my Spirit Guides, as well as my own intuitive feelings, I reached a moment of clarity where there was no more doubt about my professional future. I would connect people to the Spirit World. My mediumship work had started.

CHAPTER THREE

The Team Concept

In every incarnation, once our soul enters a physical body to experience life on planet Earth, each one of us has a "Team" that consists of a group of spirits that accompanies us from birth until death. Our Team members include our Spirit Guides, Guardian Angels, an assigned Archangel or Archangels, departed loved ones, often a specific grandparent, and sometimes a Nature Spirit or spirits. Throughout our life our Team never leaves us! They are always by our side, no matter what we do. They are there if we believe in them or not, if we acknowledge them or not, are open to their communication or are oblivious to their guidance and signs they give us. They are there if we are spiritual, religious, atheists, agnostics, or disregard or deny the Team concept altogether. Our Team is very influential during each of our incarnations on Earth. They play a significant and guiding role in our overall soul evolution. Our Team has a wide variety of missions in our life and each member of our Team helps us to achieve each goal in their own unique way, which later I will describe in detail when we discuss each specific member of our Team.

Our Team's main purpose, in general, is to help us successfully accomplish our soul's pre-designed plan. In life, our Team members are doing so by helping us to rediscover and explore our true nature as energy beings, our souls, and encourage us to stay focused on our soul's purpose and plan without taking too many "detours". In each incarnation, our Team attempts to support and guide us, progressively toward enlightenment and spiritual awareness. In this way we can learn from the major events that we experience in our life and utilize them for growth.

In each and every incarnation on Earth, our Team consists of the same type of members, but the amount of the Team members can vary from person to person depending on the nature of the soul plan in each specific lifetime. For example, if the blueprint (the life's details planned in advance by the soul) of a specific incarnation includes a lot of difficult life events or dramatic and severe experiences to balance the soul's karma, we will probably enter planet Earth with additional Spirit Guides for wisdom and guidance. If an incarnation's blueprint includes risky or dangerous experiences, we will have additional Guardian Angels to protect us. Additionally, it is important to note that throughout this life, and every life we experience, we have in addition to our permanent Team, many other Spirit Guides, Ascended Masters, various Angels, Nature Spirits, and other Light Beings that will come in and out of our life as required. When we are struck by an illness for example, experience the loss of another person, lose a job or a home, are about to embark on a risky trip, are about to get involved in a specific dangerous type of project or work, are going through a divorce, are going through depression, are feeling lost, scattered, lonely, or overwhelmed with fear, there are additional powerful and wise spirits that will join our permanent Team members and provide us with extra help, protection, guidance, support, and, of course, love.

In life, we can also be accompanied by what I refer to as the "Specialized Guides". Specialized Guides are souls that through their many incarnations on Earth have gathered a lot of experience and gained specific areas of expertise. They will then assign themselves to people that are in need of their specific skill. For example, I often observe that people who are creative, like artists and writers, will have a specialized guide near them when they do their work who helps them with inspiration, ideas, and problem solving. People who are healers and teachers in this life will also have Specialized Guides who provide them with targeted guidance in addition to their regular Team and will help adjust their energy and support their physical and mental bodies while they are helping others. These are just a few examples of the important roles that these wise Specialized Spirit Guides offer us in life when we need help with a specific task, project, or work.

There are two main rules that control the degree of help and involvement that our Team members will have in our lives. The first rule pertains to free will. As discussed earlier, in the incarnation chapter, the law of free will gives us the freedom of choice as a major part of the way we grow on Earth. Meaning, that in life the choices and actions are for us to make and no one, including our Team, is allowed to interfere, influence, or manipulate us and the decisions we make. If our Team members realize that a certain choice we are going to make is negative or harmful to us or others they will, of course, do all that is within their power to inspire and encourage us to change that choice to a wiser more positive one. However, if we are determined to pursue it anyway, our Team members will have to back off and allow us to choose the course of action and then experience the resultant consequences, whatever they might be. Whether it is positive or negative, we can grow either way depending on the circumstances.

The second rule requires our own proactive participation. In life we have to help our Team in order for them to help us. Because we are the ones who experience our life, not them, we cannot be ambivalent and do nothing and then expect them to deliver desirable outcomes in all of our life experiences.

Here are a couple of examples of this. In my work, a lot of single woman come to me and are desperately looking to meet their life partner. However, once questioned, they tell me that they do not meet many men because they are too busy to go out, are to shy, have too many home and work responsibilities, do not believe in online dating as a way of meeting a serious partner, believe online dating is not for them, or finally, simply like to stay home. These woman also say that they would like to meet a man, but are skeptical about finding love at their age, are nervous to meet someone new, compare previous lovers to new men, or do not believe that a man would love them just the way that they are now. Well, I ask you, what do you think that these women's Teams in the Spirit World could do to help them given these circumstances? Unfortunately not very much. No matter how magical and powerful your Team is in helping you meet your next life partner, if you stay at home and do not put yourself out there, they cannot compel someone to come knock on your door, this is just common sense. Also, if you are engaging your mind with a negative internal dialogue, you will create for yourself, a "negative expectation" type of energy that will block out any future potential mate. However, when you do the leg work, internally and externally, your Team will pick up the slack and will be able to work with your efforts and navigate a potential life partner toward you. This is the essence of proactive participation.

Another example situation is when you are either not working or dissatisfied with your current job. Say you are looking for a new job and you are only sending out two old resumes, or insisting that your new job be located in a very specific area or town that is close to where you live. This lack of proactive participation and closed-mindedness will obviously make it more difficult for your Team to help you. By sending strong resumes to many different companies, in a wide variety of locations, you will provide the assistance and latitude for them to help you navigate to the perfect new position. Also, in regard to this specific example, you must remember that the degree and speed of your Team's help in helping you to find your dream job is affected by a wide variety of circumstantial issues like the world's economy, lack of available jobs, or high unemployment rates, which make it even more important for you to stay flexible, realistic with your expectations, and, of course, cover all your bases by doing all the necessary legwork. In general, in order to make sure that we fully realize and utilize our Team's help in our life, we must first "walk to the door" so that they can open the right one in accordance with divine timing.

Misconceptions

Over the years, I have repeatedly heard misconceptions that people have about the concept of our Team, and I believe that it is important for me to share them with you because it will provide you with additional guidance about this overall concept.

Misconception one:

People often express to me that they are unconformable with the idea that their Team is there with them all the time and is aware of their thoughts, their personal plans, as well as watching them in their most intimate moments, like when they are naked, make love, take a shower, or involved with any other kind of private experience. Addressing these concerns first starts with the explanation that our Team of spirits are not people, of course, and so we can not impose or constrain our Team members with human traits and idiosyncrasies. If we do not distinguish the vast difference between us and them and assume that they are just like us, then the concern about privacy would be legitimate. But I repeat, they are not like us. Some of our Team are spirits that have shed their mind and Ego along with their physical body after their last incarnation, a long time ago. Others are beings, like Angels, who were created for the purpose of guidance, support, and protection. All our Team members are pure, loving, and wise, Light Beings that only have the best intentions for us. They love us immensely and unconditionally. Not the type of love that we are familiar with on Earth, a love that is contaminated with the conditions of our mind, but rather a divine love which is a pure love that only spirits can experience. Although our Team is indeed aware of our innermost and intimate thoughts, and is involved in our most personal experiences, they only use this knowledge to improve who we are, to guide and support us, to protect us, and to help our soul grow. On Earth, our Team members are happy when we are happy, content when we are content, sad when we are sad, and disappointed when we are disappointed. But no matter what, are always proud of us. As for seeing us naked in the shower, be assured that they love and accept our body as it is.

Misconception Two:

People often wonder what their Team is doing at times when nothing much is happening in life. Such as when there are no major problems or challenges, at night when they are asleep, when they just relax, or when they don't immediately need them. "Don't they get bored just standing there?" I am often asked. Well, no, they don't get bored, and they never just stand there. Throughout our life, there is never a time when we do not need our Team and there is never a time when they do not help us in one way or another. Even when we think that we are in a good place in life, content, happy, relaxed, and can handle things ourselves, when we are not in any apparent need for divine help, or sound asleep, our Team is there, helping us to have a more joyful life, helping us to become better people, inspiring us with ideas, encouraging us to be more loving and more spiritually aware, and, of course, assisting us with their ultimate purpose of helping our soul grow. Also, during every moment of our life, through our intuitive system, such as gut feelings, other people's actions or words, directed opportunities and experiences, various ephemeral signs, and many other subtle forms of communication, our Team members are constantly trying to contact us so that we know that they are there, give us guidance, and let us know we are not alone. Each member of our Team can also adjust our energy when needed, inspire us to take care of ourselves mentally, emotionally, and physically, encourage us to pursue our future goals and aspirations, inspire us to have more positive and productive thoughts, work on our negative internal dialogue, inspire us to overcome our weaknesses and shortcomings, help us overcome our Ego, replace negative thought patterns with more positive ones, and help us manifest our heart's desires. And so, as you can see, our Team are always "busy", and as long as our life continues, which means that our incarnation is not yet completed, their dedicated hard work of helping us never wanes.

Misconception Three:

People tell me that they feel guilty that they are praying and asking their Team members for protection and other life requests when they should really be praying and asking God. "Isn't it God we need to pray to, and not to any other spirit or Angel?", I am often asked. The explanation for this misconception is simple. God, with his unconditional love for all human beings, made sure that each time we enter this difficult and savage planet, that we are never alone and we are being provided with all the help, protection, and guidance that we need. Also, God is the one who created our beautiful Spirit Guides, the Angels, any other beings that surround us, and for that matter, everything in general. Furthermore, God created each one of them with their specific talent, immense power, and wisdom so that they could each help us in their own unique ways. And so there is no reason to feel any guilt. Praying to your Team members for help, protection, or healing for you and your family, is perfectly acceptable. This is why they are there. Praying for your Team's help has nothing to do with praying to God. Of course, praying directly to God is a good thing to do as well. The bottom line is that without God our Team would not exist and neither would we or anything else.

> **Fully trust and authentically believe that you are surrounded by powerful and wise Light Beings who guide, support, and protect you all the time. The more you believe in the presence of your Team in your life, the more you will be able to feel and sense their immense love for you and recognize the evidence of their existence!**

CHAPTER FOUR

Our Team Members

The Spirit Guides

Our Spirit Guides are human souls that have completed all of their Earthly incarnations and no longer need to use life on planet Earth in order to advance their soul's evolution. Through their many lifetimes on Earth they have accumulated a great amount of wisdom, knowledge, and spiritual power, as well as having balanced all the karmic debt. This enables them to remain in the Spirit World and continue their growth by becoming Spirit Guides who are teachers that provide guidance and support to human beings here on this planet. In each life, every one of us has two Spirit Guides. We each have one primary Spirit Guide and a secondary one. Our primary Spirit Guide accompanies us through the entire length of our incarnation. From one incarnation to the next, we are always accompanied by the same primary Spirit Guide. Furthermore, we do not share our primary Spirit Guide with anyone else. We each have our own who is dedicated to our growth. Our secondary Spirit Guide also accompanies us through our life. As with our primary Spirit

Guide, we do not share our secondary Spirit Guide with anyone else. Our secondary Guide usually changes from one incarnation to another. Our secondary Spirit Guides have also completed all their Earthly incarnations and therefore are equally as evolved, wise, and powerful as the primary Spirit Guides. However, the secondary Spirit Guides are not yet assigned to one specific soul. They are not yet ready to become a primary Spirit Guide and they, too, are in a process of growth so that one day they will be experienced enough to become primary Spirit Guides. Secondary Spirit Guides are in the process of learning, and are doing so by observing the primary Spirit Guide's work in order to learn the "tricks of the trade" like an apprentice. I often refer to our secondary Spirit Guides as "trainees"

When I connect a person to his or her Team, the person's trainee Spirit Guide will be less involved in the channeling and will usually stand behind the primary Spirit Guide, carefully observing the reading as if "taking notes" and studying the communication. Every once in a while, a trainee Spirit Guide will indeed offer some extra channeling in addition to the channeling provided by the primary Spirit Guide. This, however, is more of an exception than the rule. I must also say that it is very easy for me to immediately distinguish a person's primary Spirit Guide from that of their trainee Spirit Guide. The primary Spirit Guide's energy is much more authoritative like a teacher, or a concerned parent, whereas the trainee Spirit Guide appears with a softer energy. Keep in mind, however, that both our primary Spirit Guide as well as our trainee Spirit Guide are both influential in our lives. Interestingly enough our primary Spirit Guides have their own style of teaching. Obviously, they are not human anymore and do not have a mind, an Ego, or a "personality" per se. Nonetheless, their teaching styles and characteristics differ from one Spirit Guide to another. Some appear to be more strict and are very serious, especially when they feel that the information they provide pertains to the soul's path on Earth, or when the person's well-being is compromised by negative or reckless behavior. Other Spirit

Guides are more easy-going and less tough. Some Spirit Guides also appear to be more hands-on teachers and are directly involved in all aspects of the person's life. While others appear to be more in the background, allowing the person to try to handle things themselves first before rushing in to get involved. Some Spirit Guides are funny, some are talkative, and others are more quiet. Some Spirit Guides are very demanding and easily express their complaints when the person does not pay attention to their guidance and is "spiritually lazy", while others are more tolerant of mistakes and appear more patient with their expectations. Some Spirit Guides are even helpful to me, as a medium, and are mindful and take their time to help me better understand them and receive the messages during the channeling more clearly. Some Spirit Guides even guide me and offer me advice on how to improve my communication with spirits in general. Some Spirit Guides intentionally allow me to try harder and do not offer any help in order to assist me by improving my work through practice. Over the years I have come to understand that our Spirit Guide's teaching styles are all different because we are all different. It is similar to a mother or father who will most likely not use the same parenting approach to teaching all of their kids in the exact same way, but rather examine and implement the parenting techniques that are most effective with each individual child. Every life, our primary Spirit Guide adjusts their teaching style and techniques based on our specific personality's strengths and weaknesses, as well as what it is that we need to accomplish in each specific incarnation. It is very likely that in our next incarnation our Spirit Guide's teaching style will be completely different than it is in this one. I am certain, however, that in this life, as well as in any future lives, we will need our Spirit Guides to sometimes be tough with us, especially at times when we are lazy or urgently need to "wake up and smell the coffee" in life. It is important for me to mention here that despite the different styles of teaching, our beloved Spirit Guides immensely love us and deeply care for our well-being and for the success of our present incarnation. And as Spirit Guides often tell me, "Your life is our life, we are one and the same!".

Our Spirit Guides in Our Daily Life

In life, our Spirit Guides are the ones who support and guide us in our day-to-day life. Having become so familiar with life on this planet, they help us with all our relationships. The intimate relationships, the relationship we have with our parents, siblings, children, extended family, friends, and even work colleagues. Additionally, they help us with things like pursuing a desirable job or a new career, discovering our soul's purpose on Earth, as well as working through all other experiences like life-challenges and major events. As evolved, human souls themselves our Spirit Guides have incarnated thousands of lifetimes and therefore, have familiarity with every variation of life's circumstances and experiences. During their many incarnations they have experienced the negative temptations that life on Earth has to offer and are very familiar with how easy it is to get lost in them. Due to the many different forms and life circumstances which our Spirit Guides have incarnated into, such as male, female, homosexual, bisexual, white, black, healthy, disabled, rich, and poor, they have gained a full understanding of the human being's body and mind with all the complexities and limitations. Also, becoming familiar with the Ego and its negative effects, our Spirit Guides fully understand how extremely difficult it is for us to overcome its great power and how easy it is for us to remain stuck in its negativity.

As was mentioned earlier, the major events and significant people in our life are indeed pre-designed by our soul prior to the incarnation. In the course of the life, our Spirit Guides will recognize when we are stuck, spiraling down, or drifting away from our spiritual path and will consistently navigate us toward a variety of necessary experiences, events, and helpful people that can assist us to "get back on track". If, for example, our Spirit Guides recognize that anger has taken over a portion of our life and, therefore, interferes with an aspect of our spiritual growth, they can navigate helpful people toward us who will be of assistance in overcoming the anger issue. One of these people might help us overcome our anger by pointing it out to us and supporting us through the change process, while another person could actually provoke our anger in order for it to be undeniable and help us recognize it in ourselves. Our Spirit Guides might also try to "fix" our anger by creating unpleasant experiences that will cause havoc in our life in order for us to wake up and recognize these experiences as the consequences of our uncontrolled anger. Just as in the example with the anger issue, our Spirit Guides will use similar tactics to help us change other negative traits that delay or block our spiritual growth or take us further away from our soul plan, such as jealousy, envy, impatience, greed, superiority, judgment, and others. Throughout this life and every life, any negative habits, destructive behaviors, or reckless acts, will be met with faithful intervention in any way possible by our dedicated Spirit Guides. I can understand that the concept of our inherently loving and caring Spirit Guides purposely creating difficult experiences for us might sound harsh and difficult to accept. It is important, however, to appreciate that because our Spirit Guides are fully acquainted with our soul's considerable effort in designing this life so that we can utilize it for growth, they will do everything they can to help us so that we don't recklessly waste it. Conversely, in the course of our life, our Spirit Guides reward us for our participation and willingness to change. At any point, when we become pro-active about improving our life, whether it is by developing spiritual awareness through meditation, acquiring spiritual information and knowledge, connecting to spirits, alleviating our negative traits, disciplining our Ego, caring for the wellness of our physical and mental bodies, or helping others, we signal to our Spirit Guides that we are engaged and willing to change and grow. When this happens, our Spirit Guides will "kick into gear" and reward us for our efforts. They will create pleasant and helpful "coincidences" that will happen more frequently and will appear out of nowhere. Obstacles will open up for us with unexpected opportunities for better living and will occur with divine timing. Loving and helpful people will cross our path providing company, help, and support. Conflicts will suddenly and effortlessly be resolved, and greater healing energy will flow into our physical body to rejuvenate and strengthen it. We will also frequently find ourselves in the *right place* at the *right time* to accomplish, receive, or create the things that we desire. Challenges will still be there, of course, to provide potential growth; however, they will be shorter in duration and softer in intensity. In general, as a result of our efforts to grow, life on Earth will begin to flow more easily and more smoothly.

A common question I have been asked over the years is whether a person's Spirit Guides will get angry at them because they feel that their life is a mess, they have not accomplished much, they have not been nice people, or they are not spiritually aware. Unfortunately, many people can not understand how it is possible that they are so loved by their Spirit Guides regardless of the mistakes they have made in their past. My answer to these kinds of questions is that our Spirit Guides are highly-evolved Light Beings that are directly connected with the Creator's energy and so are *only capable* of expressing divine love and are *incapable* of expressing any kind of negative emotions. Additionally, our Spirit Guides will never judge or get angry at us for what we do or do not do in life, or for what we do not accomplish. How could they? After all, in one of their previous lifetimes or another, they have been in the exact same situations. However, it is important to note here that although our Spirit Guides can not express any negative emotions toward us, from time to time, they do get disappointed or frustrated with us. They are disappointed when we waste our life, do not try in any way to change, learn, grow, take responsibility for our actions, help others, or become better and more spiritual people. They get frustrated when we do not learn from our past mistakes, when we repeat the same mistakes, when we allow our Ego to govern our life, and when we are not open for the possibility of their existence.

Our Spirit Guides After Life

At the end of each Earthly incarnation, all souls, with the help of their Spirit Guides, will go through many important processes. Some of these processes will happen right after death while others will happen at a later time. Next, I will describe the processes that we all go through as souls as well as our Spirit Guides role in them.

The "After-Death" Process

At the moment of death, our soul will exit the physical body through the crown chakra, at the top of the head, and will travel through a tube or a channel, that will lead us into the Spirit World. At the end of that channel we will be greeted by our beloved Spirit Guides. It is then that we will come to the realization that our incarnation on Earth has ended and that we are back home where we are an inseparable part of the Creator. The first process that our Spirit Guides will assist us with is to once again get used to the wonderful feeling of "having no body" and to enjoy the spaceless and timeless dimension of the Spirit World. Then, they will help us to regain all our memory and awaken us from the "spiritual amnesia" that happened at the time of birth, when we forgot who we were as souls as well as our true home in the Spirit World. With this memory awakening, we will immediately recognize our Spirit Guides and recall that they are our eternal teachers and friends. It is then that we will experience a joyful and loving reunion when we will express our immense love and gratitude for their help and support that they have provided us with on Earth. At this time we will also remember the blueprint, the details of the incarnation that we have just completed, which includes the time and the manner of our death. The after-death process is a process that all souls, without exception, must go through. However, the length of this process might differ from soul to soul. Some souls might need a longer time to adjust themselves back to the feeling of having no body, and others might need a longer time to regain certain memories of the incarnation's details. Some might experience a difficult time accepting that their life on Earth has ended (commonly due to an over-identification with the mind), while others will have a hard time accepting the manner of death, especially if life was abruptly and prematurely cut short by suicide, a reckless accident, or an unexpected murder. It is important to understand, however, that no matter how difficult it might be, or how long it might take for some souls to complete the after-death process, eventually, with the help and patience of our loving Spirit Guides all souls will successfully complete it and will be ready to move forward with life in the Spirit World. Once this after-death process is completed, it is the time for our departed loved ones, the other souls with whom we have shared previous incarnations as well as all the beloved pets that we have lost, to come to greet us. This is a joyful homecoming celebration that all souls look forward to at the end of each lifetime.

The "Life-Review" Process

After each incarnation, there is another important process in which our souls require the wisdom, experience, and the expertise of our Spirit Guides.

This process is called the "life-review". In the life-review process our Spirit Guides will help us to carefully examine how much growth the incarnation has added to our overall soul's evolution. The last incarnation will be carefully compared to other incarnations to measure and analyze any spiritual growth and accomplishments. With the help of our Spirit Guides, we will review all the major experiences, relationships, successes, and failures, in order to determine how we handled them and if and how we learned from them. In this process the Ego will also be carefully examined to see how and why it interfered with our growth and what efforts were made to overcome it.

In the life-review process, karma, the "program" that helps souls balance their negative energy, will also be carefully evaluated to analyze if and how karma was used effectively. The life-review will also accommodate any new karma that was created in the course of the life by the personality. At the end of the life-review, the overall incarnation will be compared to the pre-designed blueprint to check what was actually accomplished and what was not.

The Planning of a New Incarnation

Once we are ready to enter planet Earth again for yet another incarnation, our Spirit Guides are the ones who help us with the planning of the new upcoming life. Planning a new incarnation is a very complicated and complex process that takes time to complete and requires a great deal of effort and dedication to details. A new incarnation will include not only the planning of the blueprint, but will also include all the souls that will act as major participants in the upcoming lifetime. At this point, of course, these other souls' incarnations must also be taken into consideration in order to make sure that any potential growth will be a balanced and all-encompassing benefit to those involved. While planning the incarnation's details, our Spirit Guides will help us to recognize any weaknesses that we were not able to overcome in previous incarnations and that are delaying our spiritual growth. Our Spirit Guides will help us to include these in the upcoming life for our next undertaking. Karma that was created in the previous incarnation will also be carefully added to the incarnation's blueprint in the form of life experiences so that any negative energy can be properly balanced. The process of planning an upcoming incarnation is a crucial part of our overall soul's evolution and the knowledge and the help that we receive from our Spirit Guides is fundamental.

> **Your Spirit Guides are fully aware of your incarnation's plan and will do all that they can for your highest good. BELIEVE that your powerful and wise teachers are by your side, TRUST in their help, and have FAITH in their love.**

The Angelic Kingdom

In this section I will provide a general description of Angels and their dimension. This is a very large subject and I will discuss a very brief overview of it here. There is a great deal of fascinating information on the subject of Angels outside of this text which I encourage you to research and study. Also, in this book I will be concentrating mainly on the Angels that are a part of our "Team", consisting of our Guardian Angels and the four Archangels, that I have worked with over the years and found to be the most involved and influential in our daily lives.

The Spirit World is divided into dimensions. Each dimension has a distinctive level of awareness and vibrational energy that relates to the collective "state of mind" of the spirits/beings that inhabit it. In each specific dimension, spirits have more or less the same spiritual awareness. However, the higher a dimension is, the more spiritually evolved the spirits are that live there. In the higher awareness levels of the dimensions, spirits become more energetically free with less limitation and boundaries and they move further away from the more dense dimensions like the one that is closest to planet Earth.

Also, the higher the dimension, the stronger the connections of the spirits that occupy it are to the Creator's Energy which enable them to express more of his spiritual wisdom and power. In the Spirit World, one of these higher dimensions is the Angelic kingdom, where all Angels reside.

Angels are powerful, pure energy Light Beings that are often referred to as the Creator's "messengers" and "helpers". Angels help preserve God's creation! There are an infinite amount of Angels and they have a broad range of functions in the universe. They help this planet, other planets, human beings, other beings, nature, and all other forms of existence. Just as human beings are not equally evolved spiritually and some are more awakened than others, the same is true within the Angelic dimension. There are Angels that are more advanced in their evolution and, therefore, are more powerful than others. Among the Angels, the more evolved ones have more complex functions and missions and assist the less evolved Angels to accomplish theirs. Some Angels are also new to a specific work or task and so need the guidance and assistance of the more knowledgeable and experienced Angels.

The Angels' Purposes

On our planet, Angels guard Earth inside and out. From the outside, they monitor the energy that flows around the globe, and guard the planet from any outside negative energies that can influence or harm life. When needed, Angels can also help Earth keep herself balanced and spin correctly, especially when a major natural activity or disaster occurs that can throw her off balance. From inside the planet, Angels have a lot of different tasks and purposes and they accomplish their work in a variety of ways. Of course one of their main tasks is to not only help each and every person individually, but also help humanity in general to survive and to grow spiritually.

Angels have never incarnated into a physical body to experience life as a human being. They are energy beings that have etheric bodies, and in their natural state visually appear to me as a silhouette of energy. Sometimes, however, when they choose to, the more evolved Angels can "manipulate", or use, their energy in order to take on the apparently solid form of a person or an animal so that they can fulfill a specific task or purpose. At other times, for assistance and support, they will appear in a particular form that they know human beings are familiar with. An example of this is the Archangel Michael who, throughout history, has appeared to many people as a warrior figure with a sword.

Angels' Appearance and Personality

Although Angels do not have a specific appearance like us, they do have their own unique colored energy that distinguishes them from each other which I will describe in more detail when I talk about each specific Angel. To clear up a common misconception, let me state that Angels do not have wings. Throughout our human species' existence on Earth, it is we who invented the concept of Angels having white wings. It may be because the appearance of them with wings is soothing and comforting to us. The Angels, of course, love the concept that the white, soft, wings, help to soothe and comfort us and so, when they appear to me and others who are able to see them, they get "dressed up", as they refer to it, and take on the appearance of large beings with wings. Angels, like the Spirit Guides, do not have a mind or Ego and so do not have a personality per se, the way that people have them in our world. Additionally, just as with our Spirit Guides, Angels are different from one another in the way they teach us and relate to us human beings on Earth. For example, our Guardian Angels always appear to me to be more soft spoken in general, as opposed to the Archangels, who tend to be more strict and serious. Of course their style of relating to us has nothing to do with the level of the immense love and respect they hold for our species. All Angels absolutely adore us in every way and often refer to us as heroic souls who freely choose to incarnate into this harsh planet over and over again for the sake of growth.

> **Because Angels can be playful, they love it when we express our love for them in all kinds of fun and different ways. So be creative! For example, it will make your Angels very happy if you not only call on them but also read books about them, buy statues of them, wear an Angel necklace, ring, or a bracelet. Hang a photo of an Angel in your home or have one on your computer's desktop. Listen to songs about Angels... Once again, be creative!**

The Guardian Angels

Our Guardian Angels are beautiful, wise, and powerful Light Beings. Here on Earth, they act as the protectors of human beings. More specifically, their purpose in our lives is to protect and guard us so that we remain safe and secure and *do not die before our pre-designed time.* Their protective assistance guides our incarnation through adversity in order for us to complete our life for the duration we had planned. Our Guardian Angels also try to protect us when we are faced with significant life events and experiences in order to ensure that our incarnation's blueprint will have the opportunity to unfold according to our plan.

Visually, Guardian Angels have a transparent white color. When I channel Guardian Angels, and they choose to appear to me in their innate form, as opposed to a contrived form, like a figure with wings, for example, I can see right through their etheric body, as though looking through cloudy glass.

Although Guardian Angels can be strict with us at times, particularly when they know that our well-being and safety is compromised, they naturally have a child-like, joyful attitude with a light soft energy. As a way of revealing their immense love for us, our Guardian Angels will often "take credit" for occasions when they protected us and kept us safe. Sometimes in readings, Guardian Angels will remind people of a specific, dangerous, past incident, such as a car crash, when they were miraculously kept safe and secure due to their Guardian Angel's intervention and protection.

On Earth, we each have our own Guardian Angel or Guardian Angels that accompany us from the time of birth until the time of death. In the course of our life, we do not share our Guardian Angels with other people. We each have our own. Because not all Guardian Angels are equally evolved and some are more powerful than others, each lifetime on Earth, the number of Guardian Angels that we have assigned to us, as well as the individual Guardian Angels themselves, will change from one incarnation to the next depending on the incarnation's blueprint. For example, when we are ready to enter planet Earth with a more complicated, difficult, or complex blueprint that might include a lot of dangerous experiences, or a personality that has a genetic disposition for reckless behaviors, we will most likely enter that life with two Guardian Angels as opposed to only one. These Guardian Angels will be more evolved and experienced, therefore more fully equipped to help us in handling a life with those tendencies. It is important to remember that in addition to the Guardian Angels that are a part of our "Team", in the course of every life on Earth if we ever need any extra protection, or in the case of an emergency, additional Guardian Angels that are just "the right ones for the job" will enter our life alongside our permanent Guardian Angels for a collective attempt to keep us protected, safe, and secure.

In our daily life, our Guardian Angels' help and protection cover a broad spectrum. From protecting us against "simple" experiences that might cause us minor irritations or discomfort, to guiding and rescuing us from more complex situations that involve dangerous experiences or negative people who might cause us great harm or even death. Guardian Angels are able to foresee these negative or dangerous experiences or people, as well as the outcome of certain situations that we are involved with, and so our Guardian Angels will attempt to do everything in their power to try to warn us, and, if possible, even eliminate them from our path altogether. Of course, there are many ways in which our Guardian Angels try to do their job of keeping us safe. Depending on the severity and importance of their messages and warnings, our Guardian Angels will first try to get our attention by communicating with us through a variety of signs. These include our intuition, gut feelings, knowingness, and inner voice. Often they will also use other people to deliver their messages to us as well.

Here are a few examples of how they might protect us from a possible problematic situation.

1. A new person enters your life and you have a strong sense that something is "not quite right" with him or her. **Your Guardian Angels are helping you to avoid that person.**
2. You are ready to go on a road trip and you get an uneasy feeling that you need to postpone your departure for tomorrow morning instead of tonight. **Your Guardian Angels foresee a safer road/better traffic in the following day.**
3. You go shopping at night and you have a strong "knowingness" that you should park your car closer to the store. **Your Guardian Angels are protecting you from an encounter with a dangerous person that is within proximity of the store.**

4. A few minutes after leaving your home, you hear an inner voice telling you to head back home and make sure that all the doors and windows are properly locked. **Your Guardian Angels are aware of a possible break-in and know that there is a specific window or a door that is unlocked.**

5. You are on the freeway when you suddenly experience a fearful thought or a scary vision of crashing your car which causes you to immediately slow down your driving. **Your Guardian Angels are aware of your reckless speed and are trying to help you avoid being involved in a car crash.**

Although most people do not associate these kinds of "intuitive feelings" as messages from their Guardian Angels, they often do instinctively react to them, and therefore unknowingly follow their Guardian Angels' communication. Fortunately for them, when people do not pay attention to or ignore their Guardian Angels messages, or when there is no time for an intuitive warning, they will actually *physically, mentally, and/or energetically intervene!*

Here are few examples of this kind of intervention.

1. If you think that it was you who was pressing on your car brakes at the absolute last minute, just before hitting a car in front of you, that you had not seen, think again! It wasn't you but rather your Guardian Angel who realized that an immediate intervention was needed and *physically* caused your foot to press on the brake pedal in order to immediately stop the car and save you the hassle of a "fender-bender".

2. As a person drives, and he or she is a nervous driver on a two-lane road with busy oncoming traffic, the Guardian Angels will physically reinforce, *or strengthen the grip* of the driver's hands tightly to the steering wheel in order to keep the car from swerving into the oncoming lane.

3. Guardian Angels are also the ones who help people that suffer from any sort of panic or anxiety attacks. In the midst of an attack, a Guardian Angel will try to replace negative and fear-filled thoughts with more inspiring, positive, and hopeful ones in order to reduce the negative effect that the attack has on the body's physical reaction.

4. When a person drives while overly stressed out, worried, in a hurry, upset, or fighting with another person in the car, his or her Guardian Angels will gently "manipulate" the person's energy in an effort to help them relax and *calm down* in order to stay safe.

5. When people are on the phone and fighting with someone while driving, the Guardian Angels will often interfere with the phone's reception so that the conversation will be forced to be delayed for a later time when the car is stopped. And so, if you have an angry conversation over the phone while driving and you are annoyed at the bad reception, don't jump to conclusions and blame your cell phone carrier. Stop fighting, and your Guardian Angel will remove the interference and clear up the reception again. And better yet, do not drive and talk on your cell phone at the same time and save your Guardian Angel the trouble.

6. Our Guardian Angels will also *sharpen our senses* in order to help us be more aware of our surroundings and focus on a certain situation or tasks that might need our full attention. If we happen to have a flat tire on a busy highway let's say, our Guardian Angels will not only help us to stay calm and fearless but will also sharpen our senses so that we can be more *focused and alert in the present moment*. With sharpened senses, we will hear, see, and sense our surroundings better, which will help us give our full attention to the task of replacing the tire, help us stay extra vigilant and

aware of the oncoming cars, and then, ever so safely, merge back into traffic and go home safe and sound.

On Earth, our Guardian Angels not only protect us from any external events, people, or situations, but they also protect us from our own destructive behaviors and actions. In the course of the life, our Guardian Angels will try to intervene in many different ways with destructive and risky habits and behaviors that might cause a threat to our well-being or to the well-being of other people. A person with a heavy form of addiction, for example, which is the soul's "ultimate nightmare" against spiritual growth on Earth, will be harshly intervened with by their Guardian Angels in order to cause him or her to "hit rock bottom" and "wake up". Consequences such as jail, dysfunction of the physical or mental body, illness, bankruptcy, or any other major loss like divorce, loss of home, money, job, or important possessions, will be created by the Guardian Angels in the hope that the addicted person will seek help and change their ways. In life, our Guardian Angels are also the ones who help keep our physical, mental, and emotional bodies healthy in different ways. They encourage us to eat healthy, to exercise, and to nurture our body. They inspire us to accept our body the way it is and at the age that it is. When we do not feel well they help us to pay attention to our symptoms or discomfort and help us take responsibility for our well-being by examining the body and finding out what the problem is. It is also our Guardian Angels who navigate toward us just the right doctors, surgeons, specialists, or any other health practitioners that we need, and that are the specific ones for our exact health issue that requires care.

During any given incarnation on Earth, even though our Guardian Angels are always by our side, trying to protect us from any harm, there are several important conditions and rules that they must follow when they are ready to determine what it is they can and cannot do for us and how and when to help us. All Guardian Angels are bound by these same conditions and rules. And so as difficult as it is to accept, the help that we receive from our Guardian Angels in our lives can at times be selective and conditional. Now I can understand that the concept of our loving and powerful Guardian Angels being selective and conditional with their help and protection might sound "cold" or unfair, however, it is important to remember that their selective and conditional help and involvement has a direct effect on the ways in which they help us to effectively use life on Earth for growth. Below are the descriptions of those conditions and rules.

First: The Incarnation Blueprint

During any given incarnation, the ways and the degrees to which our Guardian Angels protect and guard us, as well as the timing of their involvement in our life's events, situations, or experiences, are not measured by their love for us, or by their feelings about these events, situations, or experiences. Also, the degree of involvement is not based on whether we believe in them or not, or if we are spiritual or religious, nor do some of us have Guardian Angels that are more loving and helpful while other people's Guardian Angels are less so. The conditions that determine the extent and manner of our Guardian Angels involvement in our lives on Earth must always correspond to our incarnation's blueprint, once again, the life's details that were pre-designed by our soul. And as described earlier, our soul planned this life, and every life, solely for growth and it is our Guardian Angels who help our soul execute this plan to its exact specifications. No more and no less. Because our Guardian Angels are fully aware of our blueprint and know exactly what it is we are supposed to experience for the sake of our soul's growth, they must choose very carefully when to help us and how, and when to back off and allow us to choose for ourselves. This conditional help also includes the time and manner of our death. For example, let's say that in a specific incarnation your soul had planned to enter

53

planet Earth for short life span. Being fully aware of our soul's plan to die young, our Guardian Angels will have to allow any and all of the specific circumstances that will lead to the time of death to unfold without any interference. Meaning that they will allow us to die at the right time and in the right manner as it relates to the pre-designed blueprint. And so when it comes to when and how we exit this planet, when and how we die, our Guardian Angels *will not*, and *can not*, override or interfere with the plan of the soul for a premature death, nor can they decide for themselves to extend the life or alter the manner of death in any way.

In summary, if an incarnation's blueprint calls for our Guardian Angels protection, they will protect us, if it does not they will not. If our soul chooses an illness as a potential growth experience, our Guardian Angels will have to allow the illness to occur. If we are supposed to have a long life, they will try to keep us safe; if our soul's plan calls for a short life they will have to allow us to cross over and go back home to the Spirit World.

Second: Karma

As discussed in the incarnation chapter, karma occurs when a soul uses various life experiences on Earth as a way of balancing the negative energy that was created by the personality and is delaying its growth and evolution. In life, it is our Guardian Angels who help us go through those experiences in order to ensure that an effective karmic process occurs. Because of the importance of karmic experiences on Earth, our Guardian Angels must ensure that these experiences will play out to the exact specification of the soul's plan, regardless of how difficult or unpleasant they might be. For example, if a soul, or several souls, choose to balance their karma through a car crash, the person's or the people's Guardian Angels will not provide any protection, nor try to avoid the crash in order to allow the karmic experience to unfold. They will neutrally observe, both the events that lead to the crash as well as the crash itself, without any interference in order to respect all the souls' karmic plans. The outcome of the crash, whether one person or more people suffer minor injuries, serious injuries, or even death, will depend on the level and severity of the karma that was required to be balanced by each individual soul. In life, our Guardian Angels can not get involved in, nor prevent, even the ultimate karmic experience of one person killing another person as a way for balancing both souls' negative energies. And so, if a person is ready to murder another as a way of balancing their soul's karma, both peoples' Guardian Angels will, once again, observe the encounter and allow it to happen regardless of how sad, horrific, or tragic the event might appear. To reiterate, when it comes to paying back any Karmic debt, the soul makes the decision in advance on how and when to do it and it is the Guardian Angels' responsibility to ensure that it will happen accordingly.

Third: Free Will

In life, because the use or misuse of our *free will* has a direct effect on the success or failure of our incarnation, and therefore on the amount of growth that our soul is able to accumulate, no one, including our Guardian Angels, is allowed to interfere with how we choose to execute the right of free will. Obviously, in order to help us use our free will wisely throughout our lives, our Guardian Angels will desperately try to communicate their messages of warning, support, and inspiration to us in order to protect and keep us safe. However, if we choose to ignore their communication or are unable to recognize their messages due to a lack of spiritual awareness, they will have to honor our final choices regardless of the consequences they foresee. For example, when a person decides to drink and then drive, which is one of the ultimately selfish, and reckless choices that people make, that person's Guardian Angels will desperately try to avoid the act by trying to inspire the person to change their mind. However, if the person's desire to drink and then selfishly get behind the wheel of a car is greater than focusing on the *inner feelings of guidance* placed there by their Guardian Angels, sadly, if an accident is to occur, the Guardian Angels *will not* be able to aid with any protection regardless of how tragic the outcome may be. And so, when we choose to act irresponsibly, even our powerful protectors that shield and guard us from harmful situations as well as harmful people, will not be able to interfere with our final choices and decisions. They will try to create alternative options for a safer and less damaging outcome and will try to inspire us to consider an alternative, more responsible choice. However, once our mind is made up on a specific course of action, they will be forced to back off without any involvement or help. It is also very important for me to remind you here that although the precise time of death is indeed predetermined by our soul prior to entering the body and, despite the great amount of protection that we are provided with by our Guardian Angels, on Earth, due to free will, "real accidents" can and do occur, because if we choose foolish or reckless actions we will get hurt, harm or kill someone else, or prematurely die! And regrettably, many people succumb to this fate.

> **You are protected by your powerful Guardian Angels! However, YOU are the one who must take responsibility for your life by avoiding any reckless, risky, or just plain stupid choices that will jeopardize the Guardian Angels purpose of keeping you safe. Furthermore, it is YOU, who need to look inside yourself and attempt to recognize the guidance that is provided by your loving Guardian Angels.**

The Archangels

In this section I will provide a brief description of the general purpose of Archangels in our lives on Earth. I will mainly concentrate on the four Archangels: the Archangel Michael, Archangel Gabriel, Archangel Raphael, and the Archangel Uriel. I will describe their appearance, their "personality", and each of the Archangel's main purposes in our lives so that you will have a fundamental understanding of how each Archangel assists you and why. Later in the book, in the practical part, I will provide you with more information about these Archangels and teach you some of the ways in which you can communicate with them.

People often ask me why I mainly discuss these specific four Archangels when I teach about the "Team" concept. First, these four Archangels are the ones who introduced themselves to me when I first began to channel spirits and they continue to work with me on a regular basis when I need information and spiritual knowledge for myself, for other people, in my readings, and in my work as a spiritual teacher. Second, as the years went by, I realized that at least one of these four Archangels, always accompanies each one of us as members of our permanent "Team" and are therefore very influential in our lives. They also have a significant role in the degree of our success during each of our incarnations.

Archangels General Information

Archangels are very powerful, wise, Light Beings. Within the Angelic dimension, the Archangels are considered to be the most evolved and, therefore, the most powerful of all the Angels, even more than our Guardian Angels. In an Earthly incarnation, each of us is assigned at least one of the four Archangels. The reason I use the phrase "assigned" here is because it is the decision of each Archangel to assign themselves to a specific human being on Earth, depending on the incarnation's blueprint and the nature of the person's needs at each of the crucial spiritual growth periods in the course of the life.

Unlike our Spirit Guides and Guardian Angels, which we *do not* exchange or share with other people, throughout our lives we *do* exchange, share, and are even accompanied by additional Archangels that are assigned to our "Team" depending on what kind of assistance we need from each Archangel, as well as *when* we need their specific assistance. In one incarnation we might have only one individual Archangel who will accompany us for the whole length of the life; in other incarnations we might have several different Archangels. Also, due to their high level of awareness and great immense power, all Archangels have the ability to *divide* their energy so that they can simultaneously be with and help as many people as they need. The ability of the Archangels to divide their energy between us allows us to share the same Archangel with one another. For example, while the Archangel Michael is a member of my own Team during this life, he is also a member of millions of other people's Teams around the world.

There are a countless number of different Archangels, and each one of them serves a very specific purpose, not only on our planet, but also on other planets, other forms of realities as well as in the spirit world. In human beings' lives on Earth, however, one of the main purposes of the Archangels is to help us with our negative traits and emotions, specifically the ones that we were unable to overcome in previous lives and thus interfere, delay, or block our soul's growth. Anger, rage, jealousy, envy, judgment and superiority are a few examples of these negative traits and emotions that our Archangels will try to help us overcome during each and every lifetime on Earth. Now, at any point in the course of the life, if we are finally able to overcome one negative trait or emotion and acquire a new one, or when one specific negative aspect of our personality is getting out of control to the point where it is creating havoc in our life, additional

Archangels will join our Team in an effort to help us overcome that weakness with additional help, support, and protection.

On Earth, the way in which our Archangels communicate with us is similar to the ways in which the other members of our Team do. Again, this is accomplished through our intuitive system, gut feelings, inner voice, various signs and signals, and using other people who act as their messengers to convey their communication to us. Archangels on Earth can also use their great power to influence and "work" on our own energy, as well as manipulate or mold their own energy and take a form of a person, an animal, or an object in order to physically assist, support, or protect us when an immediate intervention is needed in a certain situation or when our negative mind becomes a threat to our safety and well-being to ourselves or others.

The Four Archangels

The Archangel Michael

The Archangel Michael stands on the right side of human beings. His energy color is light blue like the Caribbean Ocean. The Archangel Michael is the Archangel of courage and strength. He is the warrior for humanity. With his immense love for us he offers his protection to us. He fights for human beings and he wants to help us to grow individually as well as collectively. He helps to minimize suffering on our planet so that we experience less pain. Archangel Michael truly loves us and loves to be with us. Once, I asked the Archangel Michael how long it takes for him to be by our side once we call on him. His answer was, "When you breathe in and call my name, by the time you breath out, I am already by your side". It is that fast! The Archangel Michael wants our species to survive and humanity to continue on. He guards and shields us, as well as our planet, from any negative energies or harmful entities. Archangel Michael fights for us, which is why, over the years, we have adopted the image of him as a male warrior with a sword. When I channel the Archangel Michael I get the sense that he is the most *serious* of the four Archangels. Although loving, of course, he usually tends not to joke or laugh like some of the other Archangels, but rather appears to be constantly on guard, watching in all directions as if observing who and what is around. Despite his somewhat serious "personality" or demeanor, the Archangel Michael is the most informative of the four. Ever so patiently, this wise Archangel is always forthcoming with any knowledge or information that I wish to learn, know about, or am interested in. Over the years I have channeled over hundred and fifty different messages from the Archangel Michael. As a matter of fact, most of my spiritual knowledge, information, and teaching came directly from channeling this gracious and generous Archangel.

On Earth, the Archangel Michael assigns himself to human beings who have incarnated into this planet with overwhelming fears. Not the usual fears that all of us experience at one point or another as a normal part of being human, but rather the type of exaggerated fears and terror that might cause a person to become immobilized, to not function, to miss out on growth opportunities, to become spiritually frozen, or to want to die. In life, when people have these types of fears, the Archangel Michael tries to help them become less fearful and more courageous so that they can face their fears and eventually overcome them. The Archangel Michael also helps people who have a "creature of habit" type of a personality and experience fear and resistance to necessary life changes. He also helps people who are inflexible and "heavy", energetically speaking, as well as people who do not look "outside the box" of their lives and who remain stuck. With these types of fear-filled people, the Archangel Michael tries to reassure them that they are safe and secure while facing and going through any life changes. The Archangel Michael will also try to inspire them to become more flexible and "lighter" in order to not take life so seriously and to be willing to try new opportunities and exciting experiences. Being a warrior type of a Light Being, the Archangel Michael also provides us with any extra protection in life in addition to the protection that we already receive from our powerful Guardian Angels.

Call on the Archangel Michael at any time in your life when you feel that you need to be more courageous and brave. Ask him to give you the courage to face your fears, small or large. From the fear of trying out a new haircut, to the ultimate fear of dying and death. Also ask him to help you with any sort of life changes such as changing your job, your relationships, your bad habits, your negative traits, or your spiritual awareness.

> **Express your love and gratitude to the Archangel Michael. Thank him for his involvement in your life as well as his involvement in our planet. The beloved Archangel Michael appreciates it when we have a picture of him anywhere in our home. I have a large poster of him on my office wall and he loves it!**

The Archangel Gabriel

The Archangel Gabriel stands on the left side of human beings. His energy color is shiny red. Archangel Gabriel is the Archangel of strength and power. This is not the external power of the Ego that belongs to this planet but rather the internal authentic power that we all have within us. In our Earthly incarnations, the Archangel Gabriel helps us recall and rediscover the power that we inherited from the Creator, the power of our souls. The Archangel Gabriel is a "warm and touchy-feely" kind of an Archangel. He often expresses his great love for us with hugs. In my morning meditations I always get lots of hugs from him. In contrast to the very masculine energy and appearance that the Archangel Michael has, the Archangel Gabriel has both masculine and feminine energies. He has long dark hair and his face sometimes appears to me male while other times female. The Archangel Gabriel is affectionate and loving yet wise and powerful beyond words. On Earth, the Archangel Gabriel assigns himself to human beings who have lost touch with their soul, and therefore feel weak and powerless. He helps those people who have a strong identification with their Ego and with any external power. For example, people who seek power through money, work status, control, physical appearance, sex, or superiority. Once again, through the system of intuition, such as gut feelings, the inner voice, and various other signs, the Archangel Gabriel helps these people learn that external power is illusionary and interchangeable. The Archangel Gabriel assists them to de-identify with the *fake* power of the Ego and instead, identify with the *real power* of the soul. He also inspires them to grow spiritually and recall their true nature. The Archangel Gabriel is also "God's messenger". Collectively he helps connect our world with the Spirit World and individually he helps people to connect to spirits. Also, in order for us to know, sense, and recall that we are *never* alone, the Archangel Gabriel is the one who helps us be more aware of any spirit communication that we receive, either from him, The other members of our Team, our departed loved ones, or even from the Creator. In the role of a *messenger*, during my readings the Archangel Gabriel often helps me interpret any complicated or complex channeling that I have a difficult time understanding. Throughout the reading, he helps me stay more focused and spiritually connected, so that I can receive the information more easily and more effectively. On Earth, it is the Archangel Gabriel who also helps us during times of grief. When we lose someone that we love, this loving Archangel helps ease our pain. He will comfort us and work on our energy so that we stay calm and serene even in the midst of great tragedy. When we lose a person, the Archangel Gabriel helps us to recognize any signs that we might receive from the deceased person. Additionally, he helps us to sense, hear, and feel our loved ones in the Spirit World and he always tries to inspire us to believe in the continuation of the soul after the death of the physical body. On Earth, the Archangel Gabriel helps us use our loss and grief for spiritual growth.

Call on the Archangel Gabriel when you feel powerless in any area of your life, when you recognize that you are unable to connect to the real power of your soul, or when you lose touch with your true spiritual self. You can also call on the Archangel Gabriel at a time of grief, and this means any grief. Grief over the loss of a person, a pet, a job, a partner in a divorce, or grief for a dream that you wanted to accomplish, but did not or could not.

> **When you feel alone and powerless call on the Archangel Gabriel and ask him to help you remember that you are NOT ALONE! When you meditate, visualize him by your left side with his beautiful red energy and ask him to help you connect to your "Team", your departed loved ones, and other Light Beings. Exchange hugs with him and express your love to him.**

The Archangel Raphael

Archangel Raphael stands behind us and his color is emerald green, which is the color of healing. The Archangel Raphael is the healer of all living beings. Translated into the ancient Hebrew language, the name Raphael means "Re-fu-aa", or healing, in English. Over the years I have found the Archangel Raphael to be the most playful of the four Archangels. He has red hair and freckles and a beautiful child-like fun-loving energy.

On Earth, the Archangel Raphael is attracted to people who, like himself, have a child-like and light energy because they enjoy life, have fun, laugh, don't take life too seriously, and often allow their inner-child to come out and play. The Archangel Raphael especially loves to dance. Often, in my morning meditations he asks me to dance with him. Together we listen and dance to fun and uplifting music on my iPod. Speaking of fun... he specifically likes us to dance to Ricky Martin songs. Do not be mistaken; however, this child-like, fun- loving Archangel is powerful and wise beyond words. After all, he is the healer of all of God's creation.

Since the Archangel Raphael provides his healing powers to all living beings, he not only heals us, but he also heals all animals. Our pets, wild animals, snakes, bugs, birds, as well as all vegetation, house plants, garden flowers, and the food that we plant. Because of my great love and concern for the well-being of animals on planet Earth, when I teach about the Archangel Raphael I ask people to call on him and request that he provide additional healing and extra support to each of the collective animal groups, such as horses, dogs, cats, cows etc... and especially to those groups that are struggling excessively on our planet such as the dolphin group.

In an Earthly incarnation, the Archangel Raphael eases our pain and suffering and at times when we suffer from an illness or need any help with our well-being, this powerful Archangel can heal and even completely cure us. From any sort of minor symptoms or discomfort of our body or mind, such as a light headache, a cold, or a temporary low mood, to more serious illnesses or disorders, such as cancer, a heart attack, chronic pain, or deep depression, Archangel Raphael is able to help us. Being able to divide his energy, the Archangel Raphael is able to accompany and help an unlimited amount of people at the same time. Being mindful of our incarnation blueprint, the Archangel Raphael assigns himself to people who are suffering from major challenges of the physical or the mental body as a main part of their soul's plan to grow in awareness. For example, when a person enters life with a major physical disability of the body, any major genetic disorder, or any type of mental illness, the Archangel Raphael will join that person's permanent Team and will accompany him or her for the entire length of the incarnation in order to support the body and mind and assist the person with their condition or illness. Throughout these people's challenging lives, the Archangel Raphael will also try to inspire them to use their illness, disability, or disorder for spiritual growth by using their condition to becoming more patient, have more faith, practice acceptance, surrender, have trust, become more empathetic, and so forth.

It is important to understand that when we call upon the Archangel Raphael to help us or others there is never "no help". Once we call on him he *always* and immediately appears behind us ready and willing to make us feel better. However, the degree and nature of his involvement in our lives varies from person to person. Because just like the other members of our "Team", the Archangel Raphael is also bound by the same universal laws and conditions, such as free will and karma that he must take into consideration when he gets involved with our health and well-being.

In life, the degree and nature of his help with our well-being also depends on our incarnation's blueprint. If two people suffer from the same type of cancer, for example, the Archangel Raphael's involvement with these two people's illnesses might be completely different. One person's soul plan may call for using the cancer as a path of spiritual growth with the outcome ultimately being death from the illness. The Archangel Raphael will certainly be able to ease the person's pain and suffering, as well as that of the person's family and friends to provide comfort through the dying process and the death transition. But due to the soul's choice, he will *not* cure the illness and cannot prevent the person's inevitable death. On the other hand, if the other person's soul plan also uses

65

the cancer as a way of growth but with a different outcome in which the person eventually overcomes the illness and continues on living, the Archangel Raphael will again honor the soul's choice in regard to the outcome, and will help cure the person completely. When reading the two above scenarios, it is very important to remember the immense love that the Archangel Raphael holds for us; it is completely removed from the seemingly cold concept of him healing one person and allowing the other one to die. The same is true of him being selective with the degree of assistance that he can provide us when we are sick. On the contrary, because the Archangel Raphael deeply cares for our soul's evolution and growth, and therefore for the overall success of our Earthly incarnations, he must adjust his involvement in our lives according to the ways in which our soul has planned to utilize experiences, including an illness, for growth. It is also very important to keep in mind the perspective of our soul on all challenges that we might experience with our health in the course of our life. Remember, our powerful immortal soul is not afraid of cancer or any other major illness the way our conscious mind is. Nor is our powerful soul fearful of dying and death. As far as our soul is concerned, an illness of any kind is one of the most effective ways to achieve rapid spiritual awareness and overall growth, which is why in one incarnation or another, all of us are bound to be afflicted with a serious illness of one kind or another. I can understand that the concept of our soul choosing a horrible illness as a tool for spiritual growth might be difficult for a lot of people to accept. However, if you are willing to be open to the concept from the soul's perspective of using an illness as a growth opportunity, you will be able to recognize and understand what the illness is meant to teach you if you, or someone you love, becomes ill. Also, looking at an illness from a spiritual point of view will help you more easily surrender to the outcome with the full understanding that whatever happens will indeed happen for the highest good of your soul's growth and evolution.

On Earth, the Archangel Raphael also helps people who misuse their free will, and therefore create an illness or a dysfunction of their physical or mental body due to poor decisions and choices. For example, when people are engaged in drinking, smoking, drug abuse, poor eating habits, or have a long-term stress-filled lifestyle, the Archangel Raphael will come to the aid of these people and not only try to inspire them to re-evaluate their choices and take more responsibility for their well-being, but he will also strengthen their physical body so that it can protect itself from the great damage that these unhealthy habits inflict on it. However, once again, due to the freedom of choice that we all have, no matter how powerful and magical this beautiful Archangel is, and no matter how much he wants to help us to be healthy and well, the final decisions are for us to make and it is up to us to take responsibility for our own health. However, if despite his great effort to help us we still choose to remain careless or reckless about our well-being and act self-destructive and inflict damage to our body or mind, the Archangel Raphael will not be able to interfere with the consequences of those choices, regardless of how tragic they might be, and how much suffering we may have to endure. He is required to back off in order to honor our free will.

> **The Archangel Raphael is the only Archangel that you can call upon to heal others. If your child, a family member, friend, complete stranger, or your pet is ill or not well in any way, call on the Archangel Raphael and ask for his help. Then let go and observe his magical work!**

The Archangel Uriel

The Archangel Uriel stands in front of human beings and his energy color is solid white. He is very tall, has white hair, a long white beard, and, to me, resembles Santa Claus... just with a smaller belly. Translated into the ancient Hebrew language, the name Uriel mean ORR, which means Light in English, as in God's Light.

The Archangel Uriel is the Archangel of hope. He assigns himself to people who tend to become hopeless more easily because they have incarnated into a "weak" mind affected by bipolar disorder, depression, or any other mental disorders that are included in their incarnation's blueprint as a part of their soul's plan for growth. This powerful Archangel also helps people who become hopeless because they tend to view their life with a "cup half empty" attitude which negatively affects them and their spiritual growth.

In my work over the years, I have found the Archangel Uriel to be the quietest of the four Archangels. Although always gracious and more than willing to engage in any channeling, it appears as if I am the one who needs to initiate the request for the communication which is why I use the phrase "quiet" or even "shy" when referring to him in my teaching. Having said that, I have, however, found the Archangel Uriel's presence to be, by far, the most powerful of the four Archangels and combined with his beautiful white colored energy, it is truly an incredible and indescribable sight. When the Archangel Uriel appears before me I feel so serene and calm. My body become tingly, I have goosebumps, and I experience an overwhelming sense of gratitude for him, for the people in my life, and for being alive. Each and every time I interact with this magnificent Archangel I have tears of joy.

In your daily life when you lose hope for yourself, for your loved ones, for a better future, or when you are in despair and experience a "heavy" heart, mind, spirit, or when life appears no longer worth living you must call upon the Archangel Uriel. Surrender your troubling situation and emotions to him. Visualize him carrying all your worries away. When you call on him, the Archangel Uriel will "adjust" your energy so that you can feel "lighter", and therefore find some relief from your emotional state. When you are in a down mood and everything seems to be dark and difficult, the Archangel Uriel will help you view yourself as well as your life from a "cup half full" perspective. He will also encourage you to remember the good things that you have in your life such as your children, your family, your friends, your "Team", and, of course, God.

> **During our Earthly incarnations, the Archangel Uriel is like a flashlight breaking through the darkness during our difficult times. Call on him and ask him to shine God's Light on you so that it can lift you up and inspire you to become joyful and hopeful once again.**

The Archangels' Summary

When we call on the four Archangels and they each appear by our right side, our left side, behind us, and in front of us, they form a circle of protection around our physical body that shields us and keeps us safe from harm's way. Then, once we ask each one of them to help us in their own unique way, in addition to their protection, we also receive help, support, and guidance in all aspects of our lives. When calling on the Archangels, try to not think too much about how and why those four Archangels are specifically helping you, just know that they do. Do not apply any conditions to their help either. Trust that these four wise Light Beings know exactly what it is that you need according to your incarnation's blueprint, your spiritual path, the lessons that you must learn, and your overall soul's evolution. Also, you can always ask the Archangels to help you with big or small things. You never bother them or take them away from more important things. They love you and you are always worthy of their help. Believe in the existence of the Archangels and their immense love for you.

I strongly recommend that each and every day, preferably in the morning, in your meditation session or even at any time of the day, that you breathe deeply, quiet your mind, close your eyes, and call out loud on all four Archangels. First, call on the Archangel Michael and visualize him standing by your right side with his light blue-colored energy. Ask him to give you courage to face your fears, *any fears*. Ask him to help you become a more courageous and brave human being. Request that he help you and give you courage with any life changes such as your job, a relationship, bad habits, negative traits, or your spiritual awareness. Ask the Archangel Michael to protect you and keep you safe. Then, remember to express your love for him, he greatly appreciates it.

Next, call on the Archangel Gabriel and visualize him standing by your left side with his beautiful red-colored energy. Ask him to give you strength to face your life challenges and difficulties and strength to remain true to yourself and to others. Ask the Archangel Gabriel to help you recall the unlimited power and wisdom of your soul, then ask him to help you use this power in your daily life. If you experience a loss, ask the Archangel Gabriel to help you with your grief and assistance with any communication or signs that you might be receiving from your departed loved ones. The Archangel Gabriel can also help you to better connect to your Team, the Spirit World, the universe, and the Creator. Express your immense gratitude and love to this powerful Archangel and fully trust in his help. Oh, and don't forget to hug him often. As I mentioned earlier, he loves it!

Next, call on the Archangel Raphael and visualize him standing behind you with his beautiful emerald green-colored energy. Ask the Archangel Raphael to help you to stay healthy in your body and your mind. If you need specific help with any health issue for yourself or someone else, ask him specifically what it is you need of him. Then, do not allow your mind to give any conditions to his help or to control the outcome of your issues. Fully surrender to him and trust that the Archangel Raphael knows exactly what it is you need and will do all that is within his power for your highest good. Remember that the Archangel Raphael loves to have fun and loves to dance so I suggest you listen to some fun music and visualize the two of you dancing joyfully. He will greatly appreciate that. Then, express your love and appreciation for his help and promise him that you will make the effort to have more fun and playfulness in your life, to be more a light-hearted and fun-loving person.

Last but not least, call on the Archangel Uriel. Visualize him standing in front of you with his bright white-colored energy. Feel his divine and powerful presence. Ask him to give you hope when you feel alone and hopeless. On days when your mood is low and your spirit is heavy, ask the Archangel Uriel to elevate your energy and "lighten up" your mental state. Then, always express your love and appreciation for his help and for his involvement in your life. Have faith that this magical Archangel is with you.

Now I know that you might be concerned that the above daily process might take a while, especially on days when you are short on time, which often happens in life. Well, it is simply not true. Calling on the four Archangels does not take long at all and if you do it at the end of your meditation session it will only lengthen it by few additional minutes and the reward, of course, is well worth the effort. Also, once you make it a habit to call on the four Archangels and once you memorize what to ask from each one of them, the process goes even faster. It is important to remember that with any attempt to connect with spirits, practice makes it better. If you make it a part of your daily routine to connect to the four Archangels you will strengthen your connection with each one of them, you will sharpen your ability to better sense, hear, and visualize them, and you will be able to more easily recognize and witness their involvement in your life!

> **With the daily assistance, encouragement, and support of these magnificent four, the Archangel Michael, Gabriel, Raphael, and Uriel, you can overcome your fears and become courageous, align with the strength of your soul and become powerful, care for your well-being and become healthy, and remain positive and become hopeful.**

The Elementals/Nature Spirits

In the course of our lives on Earth, the Nature Spirits, some of which are also referred to as Elementals, will periodically come in and out our lives to help and support us. Sometimes, however, depending on the person and circumstances, the Nature Spirits will join a person's permanent Team and stay in their life. Later, I will explain this concept in more detail. First, I will provide a brief and general overview of the Nature Spirits, their important purpose on our planet, and, of course, their role in our personal lives.

To begin with, I want to express how much the topic of Nature Spirits, and nature in general, is close to my heart. Since I was very young I have loved animals and nature with all my heart and soul. As a child I remember picking up stray animals and bringing them home. Because we lived in an apartment building, I needed to hide them in the closets so that my parents would not find them. Some of the bigger animals that did not quite fit in the closet I actually tried to hide downstairs in the apartment building's backyard where I fed and watched over them until I found suitable homes for them. I am glad to say that I successfully sustained this "rescue operation" from the age of twelve until I finished high school at the age of eighteen when I joined the army. Over the years I always owned pets that I rescued from different shelters. Then in 1998, I met my husband Clayton, who equally loves animals and nature, in a dog park in Long Beach, California. At that time we each had two dogs. Since then, Clayton and I have continued to rescue animals and are huge advocates for animals in need and for animal rights. Nine years ago, we both felt that we wanted to rescue some of the bigger animals, and so we left the city, settled in nature, and started to rescue draft horses. Currently, we have five draft horses that we rescued from various shelters and factories around the U.S. and Canada. Our beloved horses had been used and abused for many years and so now we let them roam free around our six-acre property to allow them to feel happy and to enjoy their lives as horses. In addition to our horses we have also rescued dogs, cats, a blue and gold macaw parrot, a desert tortoise, and many fish that of course were also rescued. Loving and living in nature, Clayton and I have been accompanied by a lot of different Nature Spirits over the years who have come in and out of our lives. Currently, we have five specific Nature Spirits who are a part of both our permanent Teams. We absolutely love and adore our Nature Spirits and greatly appreciate their company. Clayton even built them small houses so they could enjoy their own space, however, their real preference is to be in our home with us.

Nature Spirits' General Information

Nature Spirits reside in the Nature Dimension/Kingdom. The Nature Dimension is the closest one to planet Earth and yet its dimension is higher in vibration than ours. This means that all the various inhabitants of the Nature Dimension, including all the Nature Spirits, vibrate at a higher frequency than us human beings which enables them to exist without a dense physical body. Having a higher vibrational frequency is also the reason most people on Earth can not see them with their eyes. Being so close to our own dimension, in addition to the many purposes that they fulfill in our world, the Nature Spirits are all around us and so they tend to mimic our behaviors and exhibit a variety of emotions that resemble our own. Because their world is so close to ours it also causes the Nature Spirits to "sponge" our energy both positive and, unfortunately, negative as well.

There is an unlimited number of types of Nature Spirits. Some of the more commonly known ones include the gnomes, fairies, elves, leprechauns, brownies, and pixies to name a few. Just like the Archangels, Guardian Angels, and Spirit Guides, the Nature Spirits also differ in their levels of spiritual awareness. Some Nature Spirits are more ancient, evolved, powerful, or more experienced with certain tasks than others. Nature Spirits also have different personalities and temperaments. Some are friendly, fun-loving, and have a child-like nature like the elves and the gnomes, for example. Others can be more guarded, serious, and even mischievous like the leprechauns and pixies. It is important to keep in mind, however, that despite their level of spiritual awareness, or different personalities and temperaments, Nature Spirits are never negative. These beautiful beings are always positive, deeply love and care for humanity, nature, and the entire planet Earth.

The Nature Spirits play a very significant role in our well-being, both individually and collectively. As a matter of fact, some of the more evolved Nature Spirits, who refer to themselves as the Elders, are so important that without them our planet would not exist and therefore neither would we. Why is this? It is because of the Nature Spirits, called the Elementals, who are divided into four groups and are responsible for tending to the four different forces of nature.

Their purpose is to help sustain the four elements: earth, air, fire, and water.

The Nature Spirits that maintain the *earth element* are the ones who protect all plants, flowers and trees, nurture them and allow them to grow in order to serve their unique purpose. They also help to enrich our soil with various minerals. These beautiful Nature Spirits also cleanse our planet from any dangerous pollutants that are harmful to our well-being. On a more personal level, they help our gardens flourish, they help farmers with their work and livelihood, and even help our home flowers to stay fresher and alive longer.

The Nature Spirits that are responsible for the *air element* help to clear planet Earth's atmosphere from any toxic influences such as man-made ones from automobiles and factories. They also help to purify the air that we all breath and allow it to flow more easily. They help us to better utilize the magnificent gift of breathing for improving the well-being of our body and mind. On a larger scale, they are responsible for maintaining natural forces such as wind, hurricanes, tornadoes, and the trade winds to mention a few.

The Nature Spirits that are responsible for the *fire element* help to use the energy of our souls to form our reality in our physical world. They also help to sustain the energy, the Chi, that "feeds" all planet Earth's inhabitants and helps to sustain all life with the power of spirits. These Nature Spirits also help humanity to wisely use fire, gas, electricity, and light in daily life.

And finally, the Nature Spirits that are responsible for the *water element* help sustain and support all oceanic life and all other lives that are in other water environments such as lakes, rivers, etc. This Nature Spirit group also helps to purify the water that we use from any toxins, poisons, or pollution that might harm us or any other living beings. They even help the water within our bodies to properly nurture it and keep it healthy.

The beautiful hard work of the Nature Spirits also helps our planet and humanity in a variety of spiritual ways. It is the Nature Spirits who help absorb the negative energy that human beings are projecting out into the planet's atmosphere by their individual and collective Egos' destructive choices and actions. The Nature Spirits also try to protect planet Earth from the negative energy that human beings create when they dishonor and mistreat her. Examples of this can be seen in the destruction of the rainforests, the mistreatment of the animal kingdom, the careless attitudes toward the planet's cleanliness and in the disrespect for the ocean and its inhabitants.

On the human beings' collective level, the Nature Spirits help clear some of the negative energy that is imprinted on humanity through previous and current wars, murders, torture, and other major destructive actions that human beings have inflicted on one another throughout history. On an individual level they try to help purify people's mental state from their Ego's negative emotions such as greed, envy, rage, resentment and many others. And so, as you can see, these beautiful beings are very important to our existence as individuals and as a species. They are important in our personal lives, our world, and, of course, our planet.

Unfortunately, due to the harsh nature of our world at the present moment, the destructive collective Ego of humanity that appears to "lead the way" with a general disrespect toward nature, it is taking a toll on the Nature Spirits who are exhausted with the amount of work both spiritually and physically that is required in order to help us and the planet. They are also overwhelmed with the massive amount of negativity that they are attempting to clear up and the amount of negative energy that they must absorb as well. Because of this, the Nature Spirits certainly need our help. We can help them by minimizing the amount of negativity that we project into the world and, of course, by the way we care for and respect nature. The Native American cultures, for example, were well aware of this relationship with the Earth and because of that, they were both great stewards of the environment and lived in tune with nature and had actual communication with all of nature.

Beside helping to support the Nature Spirits, there are other important reasons for caring and honoring nature. The first reason we must respect and love this planet is because we do not own it. It does not belong to us, we are merely visitors here who one day will leave this place and make room for someone else to enjoy this magnificent blue planet. Finally, and most importantly, when we love, respect, and honor nature, we do so to God's creation and to do so to God's creation is essentially doing the same to him!

Nature Spirits as a Part of our Team

In our day-to-day personal lives the Nature Spirits help us in many ways. While not as powerful as the other members of our Team, they are equally magical in the ways they help us. The Nature Spirits provide us with help and support for all kinds of different problems, challenges, or experiences that we might face. Although these experiences are simpler and less complex than the ones we are assisted with by the other members of our Team, the help that we receive from our Nature Spirits, however, makes our lives run more smoothly, more enjoyably, and certainly with less frustrations. For example, the Nature Spirits often help us find things that we have misplaced or even lost. This unique assistance they provide helps us find things like our car keys, TV remote, cell phone, wallet, or a piece of jewelry that we thought was long lost. The Nature Spirits in life also help in a variety of fun ways. They help us find good parking spaces that are closer to the store, like our Guardian Angels do or, when we drive, they like to help us "catch" all the green lights and miss all the red ones. When traffic is heavy or stopped they often help get it moving so that we will not have to rush, miss an engagement, appointment, or a meeting. Our Nature Spirits especially enjoy helping us with any electronic devices that are partially broken or are no longer functioning, such as our computers, alarm clocks, microwaves, washer and dryer machines, or jacuzzi to name a few. Over the years the five Nature Spirits that accompany Clayton and me in our lives have fixed many different devices in our home. Their latest help was with my treadmill. It was acting erratically and was slowing down and speeding up unpredictably. I asked my Nature Spirits to "take a look at it" and try to fix it which they immediately did. My treadmill has been functioning normally ever since.

It is important to know that not all human beings necessarily have the Nature Spirits as members of their permanent Team. The reason for this is because their involvement in people's lives can be somewhat selective in whom they choose to accompany. This is due to the type of energy they have as well as their picky nature. Also, the interaction that Nature Spirits have with people varies from person to person. Let me explain what I mean. Naturally, the Nature Spirits will be energetically attracted to people who love and respect nature, animals, and Gaia, our Mother Earth. And so, when we authentically love and respect nature with all its forms we will be accompanied by these beautiful beings and enjoy the magic they create for us. On the other hand, people who do not respect, care, or honor nature, create a type of energy not compatible with the energy of the Nature Spirits which will make any interaction with them unlikely to occur.

In the course of my work with the Nature Spirits over the years I have been told that due to the mischievous nature of some of the Nature Spirits they can, and will, actually cause some discomfort and unpleasant occurrences in the lives of people who are intentionally destructive to nature in general, such as people who commit arson, exhibit cruelty to animals, or carelessly pollute the environment. Also, due to the spiritual concept of the "law of attraction", Nature Spirits tend to be energetically attracted to people who are similar to their own energy, level of awareness, and to people who resemble their own personality and temperament. This is why the *kind* of Nature Spirits that accompany people can vary from person to person. For example, fun-loving, playful people, will most likely attract the elves into their lives, while energetically "heavy" and guarded people will most likely attract the leprechauns. Also, in the course of our lives as we change and spiritually grow we are able to invoke the more evolved, powerful, and experienced Nature Spirits.

In order to invoke the Nature Spirits into your life and enjoy the great help and support that they can provide you with, make an effort to love, respect, and honor all of nature. Respect and care for all animals. Help them live their life happily doing what it is they are meant to do and do not treat them like second-class citizens of this planet, because they are not! Each and every one of them has a significant contribution to make and an important purpose for us and to this planet. Also, express your love for Gaia by respecting the planet in every way. Do not throw cigarette butts or garbage out of your car window. When you go to the beach, enjoy the ocean and the beautiful sand but keep it clean when you leave. When you are out in nature leave things the way they are. Don't interrupt or interfere with anything. "Take nothing but pictures; leave nothing but footprints".

Believe in the existence of the Nature Spirits! Pay attention to your life's little miracles that are created by the Nature Spirits who accompany you. These miracles might be plain and simple but are there to help your life run more smoothly and joyfully. Also, Nature Spirits greatly appreciate it when we acknowledge them and hold gratitude and appreciation for their support, hard work, and dedication to the well-being of our species, our world, and our planet. So take a moment and thank them often!

Our Departed Loved Ones in the Afterlife

In addition to our Spirit Guides, Archangels, Guardian Angels, and possibly the Nature Spirits or Elementals, some of us might also have a specific soul of a friend or a family member that will join our permanent Team and accompany us throughout our life. In this section I will explain how and why this happens. First, however, I would like to discuss soul mates. I believe that this is a very important concept to fully understand not only because it will help explain some of the information in this chapter, but also because the concept of soul mates relates to many other spiritual topics.

Soul Mates

The phrase "soul mate" has been greatly misused and misunderstood and, therefore, has lost its spiritual meaning which is why, during the course of my work, I come across so many people who are confused about who and what soul mates are. These people often fantasize about the term soul mate and ask themselves questions such as, "Where is my soul mate?", "Why haven't I found them?", or "Is the one I am with, *the one*?" The term soul mate is often casually tossed out in everyday conversation with the intended meaning of describing a single other person, usually an intimate lover, that is "out there" or "with us" and the term is wrapped in romance and mystery. People think of a soul mate as a specific other person, usually an intimate lover, who will enter their life in order to make them happy, fulfilled, and complete. That imaginary soul mate person will accept and love them unconditionally and will spend the rest of his/her life with them and they will live happily ever after. A person so perfect in every way that they can only be some character from a romance novel. Unfortunately, from the perspective of our souls, soul mate has a completely different meaning from the description above. I hope that by sharing the information I have learned from the Spirit World in regard to soul mates that I will be able to clear up some of the confusion and give you a clearer and broader picture of what this whole concept is about.

In the Spirit World souls are divided into clusters of small "soul groups" that are usually between eight to fifteen souls. The members of each soul group are considered to be soul mates. Our immediate soul group is extremely important to our soul's evolution. Each group of soul mates knows each other since the creation of each soul and, therefore, is fully aware of each other's spiritual evolution. The spiritual awareness of all soul mates in a particular group is somewhat similar because even if some souls grow faster and become more evolved they will always help the others to "climb up" to their level in order for the whole group to continue to grow together. The love that soul mates share with one another is eternal and indescribable because it is a pure divine love. It is the kind of love that we can never experience here on Earth due to the limitation of the physical mind.

For the most part, once we belong to a specific soul group we do not move to another group. We grow together as a group. That does not mean that we as souls in the Spirit World are not involved with souls belonging to other groups. On the contrary, reflecting our "God-like" beautiful loving nature, all human souls are dedicated to the spiritual growth of one another. It is only the manner and pace at which we grow that has to do with our immediate group.

There are various ways and places in which soul mates help each other grow. Sometimes some soul mates within the group decide to incarnate together into planet Earth while the rest of the group stays in the Spirit World and assists the ones that are experiencing an Earthly incarnation. It is also common that every few lifetimes the whole group might decide to "take a break" from incarnating all together for a while and stay in the Spirit World to grow from there. If some of this is confusing, let me try to illustrate it simply with a scenario I have been shown from the Spirit World. Imagine a large table in the Spirit World and a group of ten souls alongside their primary Spirit Guides gathered around it in order to plan their next incarnation on Earth. These soul mates will be planning life scenarios that will help them overcome spiritual obstacles that they were not able to achieve in past incarnations. Each soul will have different challenges to overcome in the next lifetime. These souls around this imaginary table will work together planning who they will be, what they will do, and most importantly how they will manifest in each other's coming incarnation to best help one another. Once the incarnations have been formed and each soul member of the group has been assigned to a particular relationship with one another, the agreement is bound by a "soul contract" which includes all the major details of the experience. For example, a soul contract between parents and children will include certain childhood experiences, both pleasant and unpleasant, the energy and personality of the mother and father as it relates to the children, the nature of the upbringing, and the culture and circumstances of the family life, among many other details. A soul contract between life partners will include the divine timing when the partners are suppose to meet, the type of relationship, whether it be homosexual or heterosexual, the nature of the relationship as it relates to each soul's specific lessons, whether or not the partners are supposed to produce any children, and so forth. Soul contracts among soul mates will also include all the details of the potential lessons and challenges that everyone is supposed to learn for the sake of the soul's growth and evolution. The length of the contracts that we have with each specific soul mate relates to the type of experiences that we are supposed to accomplish together as well as the degree of success or failure of achieving those experiences.

In life our soul mates might take the form of intimate lovers, siblings, parents, children, family members, as well as close friends, and the relationships can manifest as significant ones that end either poorly, fine, or even tragically. And once again the relationships can be short-term or long-term. Our soul mates might also take the form of someone that we do not necessarily like or even love. Regardless of the form our soul mates take, each incarnation they are all a crucial part in our journey on Earth and are significant to our soul's evolution. On Earth, however, not all the significant people in our life are necessarily our soul mates. For example, in your family, your mother may be your soul mate or from the same soul group, while your father may not be. That does not necessarily mean that because your mother is your soul mate that you love her more, are supposed to care for her more, or have a better relationship with her than with your father. From a spiritual perspective being a soul mate with your mother means that the potential lessons you must share in the course of your lives are far more important and are a greater contributor to your soul's overall evolution than with your father's soul. Being a soul mate with your mother also means that both your souls can help each other with balancing any negative karmic debt from previous lives. In the previous scenario, your father obviously has an important role in your life as well or, otherwise, your souls would not have chosen to incarnate together into the same family. This is why any experiences you had or have with your father, good or bad, easy or challenging, from childhood to adulthood, should be fully cherished and valued as equal to the experiences you had or have with your mother. The previous scenario will help you understand that it is not important to know whether one person in your life is your soul mate while the other one is not. From the perspective of your soul, all your relationships are, of course, important to everyone's evolution. Even though it is not important to try to figure out who your soul mate is in life and who is not, there are two ways in which you can tell. First, you can intuitively feel the depth of the different connections you have with the people in your life. With a soul mate the connection, good or bad, is powerful as well as influential on your life. The reason I use the word *intuitively* is because if you rely on your emotions to determine if someone is your soul mate your personality will judge that decision based on the experiences that you shared with the person. If the experiences were difficult, challenging, unpleasant, or hateful, you will most likely decide that "there is no way that he or she could possibly be my soul mate". However, an intuitive feeling is an inner sense that is governed by your soul and has nothing to do with the nature of the relationship or with the person. When you are aligned with your soul and rely on your intuition and inner sense you can more easily detect your soul mates in life. Another easier and more obvious way to tell if a new life partner is a soul mate is by evaluating the partnership to see if its an "Ego relationship", as I call it. This means that if you decide to get involved in a relationship based solely on your Ego's external reasons, such as the partner's good looks, amount of money, or social status he or she has, or if you get involved in a relationship due to your fear of being single or the desperate need to get married, then you have your answer. The person will most likely not be your soul mate because soul contracts between soul mates are never based only on Ego fixations. Having said that, it does not mean that our soul mates in life can not be good looking, have money, and be successful. It simply means that these characteristics were not our soul's *only* reasons why we are together. Another important point here is that even "Ego relationships" can be used by both people's souls as a potential motivation for necessary changes, for growth, for spiritual awakening, and ultimately for the soul's evolution.

In summary, use the concept of soul mates in order to honor and value all the people in your life equally. Learn from all the experiences that you have with each and every person that you share your life with or that cross your path. Try to carefully examine what these experiences are meant to teach you and how they contribute to your soul's growth. Learn from any "red flags" that you ignored and any mistakes that you made in your previous relationships and apply these lessons to your current or future relationships in order to improve them. When you carefully review your past and present relationships, happy or difficult childhood, loving marriage, devastating breakup, loyal friends, and the friends who betrayed you, you will realize how they were all important factors that have contributed to who you are today. Also, be certain that some of these people that shared these significant experiences with you are your soul mates and they have all contributed to your soul evolution and growth.

A Departed Loved One in Our "Team"

The people that we love and miss so much that have passed away are not dead. In fact, they are more alive than they ever were because their immortal souls are back home in the Spirit World where they are whole again, joyful, and in peace. From the Spirit World our loved ones can see and hear us and are fully aware of us and of our lives. This is particularly true immediately after death when our loved ones will constantly be with us in order to help us during the time of grief after their passing. Eventually, however, as time goes by, their soul will leave our side in order to move on with their pursuit of growth, but periodically will continue to come in and out of our lives when we call on them, when we miss them, when we need their help and support, on special occasions such as birthdays or anniversaries, special holidays, or just in order to "check up" on us.

A departed loved one who chooses to join our permanent "Team", on the other hand, will never leave us. They will accompany us throughout the length of our incarnation until our own time on this planet ends. Due to the free will that we have in this world as well as in the spirit world, each soul, after death, can choose whether or not joining their loved one's Team is the best thing for them to do at that time, spiritually speaking. The decision of a soul to join its loved one's Team is based on a variety of reasons and, each of which, determines the degree and manner of the help and involvement that the departed loved one's soul will have in the person's life on Earth.

The following are some of the main reasons.

An Unfinished Contract

As discussed earlier, soul mates have a soul contract with one another. Sometimes, however, a soul contract that we have with another soul mate might not quite go as planned and the soul contract "expires" or ends. On Earth, a soul contract with a soul mate will expire once the experiences have added sufficient growth to the soul's awareness, or, conversely, if growth becomes impossible to achieve due to the Ego and the negative nature of the person's choices. In other words, any relationships that we have in life, whether it is with our soul mates or with other souls, are only designed to help advance the soul's awareness and, if that is impossible to achieve, for whatever reason, the souls will move on and will create other potential growth experiences. Once a soul contract expires, and the person who contributed to the failure of the unfulfilled contract dies, the soul will have the opportunity to make things better and complete the contract by joining the surviving person's Team and help him/her from the Spirit World.

Here are a couple of examples that will help you understand what I mean:

When two soul mates enter planet Earth with a soul contract as a *husband and wife* and, in the course of the marriage, the husband has an affair, leaves his wife and family for another woman then dies either right away or years later. From the Spirit World his soul will have the opportunity to choose to join his wife's Team in order to fulfill his obligation to the contract and become the husband that he should have been and never was. Being an additional member of his wife's Team, he will accompany her throughout her life helping her to forgive him, to live her life according to her incarnation's plan, and to spiritually grow. He will also protect and guard his wife and even help navigate toward her a suitable partner, assuming that she has another soul contract planned. Or when two soul mates enter planet Earth with a soul contract as *close friends*, and through a reckless action one of the friends causes a tragic accident that kills them both and ends their soul contract prematurely, after death, the soul of the person who caused the accident will have the opportunity to join the Team of any member of their friend's surviving family such as the spouse, children, or parents, in order to once again become a supportive friend.

The Blueprint

Sometimes, after death, the decision of a soul to join a person's Team is already included in the incarnation's blueprint that was created by both souls prior to entering life. For example, when two soul mates enter planet Earth with a soul contract of being twin sisters and one of them has a pre-designed life span of eighty years while the other has a pre-designed life span of eight, the incarnation's blueprint of these souls might include the soul of the sister who exits life first to join the surviving sister's Team in order to provide her sisterly love, support, and guidance for the rest of her life.

Grandparents' Love

Over the years, in my work, I have often witnessed grandparents joining their grandchildren's Team. When I ask the souls why they chose to do so they have explained to me that on Earth grandparents and grandchildren have an intense connection, a special bond, and a very important and unique soul contract that often continues after death when they join the grandchild's Team. And so basically the role of a grandparent in the grandchildren's Team has to do with love. That same intense love that they shared in life continues on after death. From the Spirit World, when one of our grandparents is a part of our Team, they will love and support us when life is difficult. They will soothe our energy and uplift us when we don't feel well. They will keep us company when we are lonely and will support and guide us with the raising of our own children. They will even accompany us in the kitchen to inspire us to cook some of the delicious recipes that we shared with them in life, assuming we can cook, of course. In the course of a life, a grandparent will sometimes skip from one grandchild's Team to another's as needed. For example, a grandmother might join a grandson's Team for a few years, then will switch to her granddaughter's Team when she is ready to become a mother in order to provide extra support with raising the new baby. In my own life, my grandmother Clementina, joined my permanent Team when I entered my spiritual path. Alongside the other members of my Team, she helps and supports me in my work as a medium, especially in readings. When I do group readings and large events my grandmother Clementina is my organizer. When there are a lot of souls who wish to come through to participants she lines them up in an orderly manner based on the priority and importance of the channeling. My Grandmother also provides me with extra energy and support when a specific reading or event is overly draining.

Karma

Souls can also choose to join a person's Team as an opportunity for balancing any negative karma that was created in the course of their life. For example, if due to reckless driving, a person died in a car crash and that crash also involved another vehicle in which the other person survived, yet was severely hurt and became paraplegic, the reckless and irresponsible choices of the person who caused the crash would have created negative karma for his/her soul that now must be balanced. One of the ways in which that soul can choose to balance its karma is by joining the paraplegic person's permanent Team and help support his or her difficult life as a disabled person for the rest of their incarnation.

People often wonder how it is possible that people who loved them so much in life such as their mother or their spouse would choose *not* to be a part of their Team and continue to accompany them for the rest of their lives. Of course the answer to this legitimate question depends, once again, on who is asking. The mind or the soul? From the perspective of the mind it makes perfect sense, of course, that if we lose our mother for example, that she will immediately choose to accompany us throughout our life alongside the other members of our Team. However, from the soul's perspective, on Earth our mother was one of our soul mates that had a soul contract with us and when she left this planet the contract ended. Now in the Spirit World she is not our mother anymore. She is a soul that still deeply loves us, even more so than when she was on Earth, but she must continue to pursue her own growth process in any way she chooses to. And if being a part of our Team does not best support her growth process, the soul will make the choice that does. She will, of course, continue to come in and out our lives to provide help and support but will not remain for long in the same way the other members of our Team do. It is also very important to remember here that as souls we are all one. As souls we love each other always and forever and without any conditions. And although our loved ones in spirit always help us at one point or another in our lives it is up to each soul to choose if joining a permanent Team is best for their growth at that point in their overall soul's evolution. The choice of our departed loved ones to join our Team or not, can not be looked at as a good or bad choice. Nor can it be interpreted as the degree of love they have or had for us. Also, once a departed loved one is a member of our Team, the support, guidance, and protection that they provide us with not only helps *us*, but also contributes to their *own* soul awareness and growth, and their own evolution. This is because whenever our souls interact with and help one another in our life on Earth, the after life, and in other dimensions, there is always plenty of potential growth for all of the souls involved. The bottom line is that growth is never one-sided.

If you consider yourself to be a spiritual person you must fully and authentically believe in life after death! If you debate this concept you become "half spiritual". And that of course does not exist, in the same way that you cannot be "half pregnant"! When it comes to spirituality, you either are, or you are not.

CHAPTER FIVE

Signs

In this chapter I will be discussing the general concept of signs from spirits. I will also cover the specific signs that each member of our Team gives us and I will help you understand how to recognize, interpret, and apply the signs to your life.

In life, our beloved Team communicates with us through signs. They show us signs in order to convey their messages to us. The various members of our Team use signs to guide us, support us, warn us, and even have fun with us. In our daily life it is up to us, however, to pay attention to the signs that we receive from them and then use the wisdom of our soul to correctly interpret those signs. Of course, the more spiritual we are, the more open we become to the concept of signs from spirits in general. Being open to that concept can also help us to recognize them and more easily understand their meaning. Unfortunately, due to the nature of our world at the moment, a lot of people are busy, stressed out, scattered, over-think, over-worry, over-analyze their lives, and most people miss the signs that their Team members show them on a daily basis.

When that happens and we are too consumed with the details of life and overlook the signs, our Team will do all that they have in their power to help us slow down our energy so that we are able to stay more focused on our surroundings and recognize their signs. Then, once we are aware of the signs, through our intuitive system and gut feelings, our Team will help us to understand their meaning. Unfortunately, however, when we are mentally, energetically, and spiritually closed to their help there is not much that they can do about it and signs will be missed.

On planet Earth our Team can use unlimited types of signs and each one of those signs has a different meaning. Of course, when our Team members show us a sign they must take into consideration our spiritual awareness, our "openness", our personality, as well as the way in which we process information. Knowing us this well, however, they can easily apply all those conditions and come up with just about the perfect sign that will deliver their message to us most effectively. Of course, not all signs that we get from our Team members necessarily have a critical importance or significant purpose for us or for our life. Some signs are simply playful and fun and are being shown to us in order to lift up our spirit and mood while other signs act as a way for them to tell us that they are nearby and that they are aware of us and of our life: that we are not alone! All signs, however, no matter what their meanings are, are an expression of the great immense love and deep caring that they hold for us human beings.

Concept of Signs Rules and Regulations

Believing IS Seeing

When it comes to signs from spirits, believing is seeing. As with any spiritual concept, idea, or information in this book, it is very important that you must first authentically believe in the concept of signs and stay open-minded, spiritually speaking, to the idea that your Team members are trying to use signs as a way of communicating, guiding, and connecting with you. Having an open spiritual mind will help you to see more and miss less of the signs that your Team are showing you. Also, each day, the more effort you put into recognizing signs from your Team, the more creative you will become in interpreting them and in understanding their meaning. Then, once your Team is aware of your effort to communicate with them through signs and once they realize that you are recognizing and understanding them, they will get excited that a channel of communication is being established and will generate even more signs. Magical signs that will be clearer and more obvious to see and understand. On the other hand, if you remain close-minded and allow your mind to think too much about the validity of this spiritual concept, all the information in this chapter will be meaningless to you and frankly will be quite useless.

Recognizing signs and understanding their meaning comes from the inspiration of our Higher Self: our soul, and not the interpretation of our mind. Our mind does not understand, believe, or acknowledge, signs from spirits. If we see a sign and allow our mind to think too much about it rather than going with the immediate "knowledge" of our soul, we will come up with all sorts of explanations, reasons, and excuses as to why the sign is there and what it means. In life, our mind is the biggest obstacle to enjoying communication with our Team through signs which is why the more we think the less signs we will identify. For example, a closed-minded person that thinks too much will walk down the street, see a penny on the ground, and think that the penny was just coincidentally dropped there by another person. Also, because of how the Ego works, the person will most likely not even bother to pick it up since its "only a penny and not a quarter". A more open-minded and spiritual person that comes across a penny in the street will not only pick it up but will immediately be open to the concept that the penny is a sign from spirits. This person will probably pick up the penny, examine it carefully, take it home and keep it in a safe place and cherish it forever. Now depending on the person's spiritual awareness, he or she will also be able to intuitively know who is showing them this sign, as well as its specific meaning.

Ask and You Shall Receive

In our life, most of the signs that are being shown to us are initiated by our Team members. However, we can ask our Team to show us a sign as an answer to a question or for guidance that we might need in our life. When you need the help of your Team and want them to show you a sign it is always a good idea to be as specific as possible in what you ask and need from them. However, it is not a good idea to be specific as to the kind of sign that you would like them to show you or when the sign should appear. When you ask for a sign, it is important to leave it to your Team to generate the specific signs that they want to show you as well as the timing. Remember how wise your Team members are and how well they know you. Trust that they can effectively use this planet and your life for delivering their signs. For example, let's say that you were offered a new job and are planning to leave your current position to take the new position in the new company. You want to ask your Team to show you a sign that will reassure you that your plan for switching the company or job is something that is good for you and for your future. When you ask for the sign make sure that you are not overly specific in what type of sign you would like them to show you, just ask for a sign. Then surrender the request to them and trust that a sign will be coming your way. In the next week or so stay spiritually open, alert, aware, extra observant, and look for the sign. Once you recognize it, thank your Team and follow their guidance without hesitation.

In summary, each and every day, look for signs, the ones that are being shown to you by your Team, as well as the ones that you have asked for. When you recognize a sign use your intuition to try to understand its meaning and use this information to better your life as well as to strengthen your connection with your Team. Once you get a sign and understand its meaning, pay attention and sense how joyful and blessed it makes you feel. Each time you get a sign, any sign, thank *all* the members of your Team. Even if you know who specifically provided you with the sign, it doesn't matter. Include everyone in your gratitude.

Signs from our Spirit Guides

Because our Spirit Guides are human souls who used to incarnate into this planet and are also the ones that are most involved in our day- to-day life they often use our everyday situations, experiences, and objects that are familiar to us for revealing their signs. Our Spirit Guides use signs for many different purposes. Some signs are designed to guide us in a specific direction that we need to take or a decision that we need to make, such as a move or a new job. Some signs are designed to open a door or opportunity for us and encourage us to "walk through it". Some signs are being shown to us as an answer to a specific question or request that we asked of them while other signs are simply designed to reassure us that they are nearby and that they love us. Below are some of the most common signs that our Spirit Guides show us, as well as an example of how they might use these signs to communicate with and help us. I am hoping that by describing these few examples it will help you understand the concept and apply it to your own life.

Television Signs

Our Spirit Guides often show us signs through our television in commercials, movies, and particular programs. For example, assume we are planning to move. And since a move is an important event in our life our Spirit Guides are very influential on the timing of the move, the location, and of course, the home itself. In order to help us they may use signs on the television that will validate our move and that will show us that they are aware of and supporting us though the moving process. Sometimes through signs on our television, they will express their preference for the type of house that will be good for us as well as the location. Here is what I mean. We are watching television and happen to tune into a program that shows people moving to a new home. In that program we recognize some hidden messages that are helpful to our own move. For example, the program shows people moving from the city to nature, to a specific town, state, or country, or to an apartment, a single home, or a ranch. To help us in our move our Spirit Guides might also show us signs through commercials about the housing market, moving companies, or real estate agents. Once again, however, in order to recognize any signs on the television like the above examples, we are the ones who must first recognize them and then intuitively find out their meaning and how they are meant to help us.

Radio Signs

In the same way that our Spirit Guides use television to show us signs, radio is also an effective tool for them to get their messages and guidance across to us. If you pay attention you may happen to tune in to a certain station, song, or commercial on the radio that will mean something to you, help guide you, or give you the answers that you need. For example, I remember few years ago, one day when I was driving my car and felt alone and disconnected from the world, from my Team, and from the Creator. I asked my Spirit Guides to show me a sign that would help me feel better. I was listening to an oldies' music station when all of a sudden I was inspired to switch stations. The next station the scanner button hit was a religious station. However, the program that I tuned into was so spiritual and so beautiful. The host was quoting from the Bible. The message was about God's unconditional love for us human beings and about the miracle of life. He continued talking about the goodness of humanity, about the importance of loving one another, and about the unique purpose that we each have here on this planet. Basically he was talking about things that I knew, things that I believed in, and concepts that I lived by. However, listening to that talk radio program at that specific time was exactly what I needed to hear. I cried from joy and was thankful for the uplifting sign and for the love of my Spirit Guides. That was such a truly magical sign that has stayed with me ever since.

Songs and Musical Signs

Songs and music are used by our Spirit Guides to deliver a specific message to us but more often they use music to lift our spirits up, tell us that they are around, that we are safe and not alone, and of course that they love us. So in our daily life we must pay attention to songs and music. I am not talking only about the songs and music that we listen to in our car, but also in public places such as in the elevator, the supermarket, the doctor's office, and any other places that might have music in the background. For example, pay close attention to days when you have a specific song stuck in your head and you are unable to get rid of it. Write down the name of the song, the name of the singer/band, as well as what the song is about, but most importantly go online and find all the song's lyrics. Then examine everything that you received. Unless its an obvious love song that expresses your Spirits Guides love for you, look for their message in the song's title, lyrics, and or the meaning of the song. Once again use your intuition and the wisdom of your soul to understand the messages that are embedded in the song, as well as how it relates to your life. Our Spirit Guides will also use songs and music to lift up our spirits on days that we are down, feel hopeless, or simply in a bad mood. They will navigate a specific song for us to hear that will remind us of more joyful times. Perhaps a song from our childhood or teenage years when we felt happy and carefree.

When that happens, when that certain song comes on, sense how the energy of the song sweeps you up and lifts your mood. Use the song to change your mood. Crank up the volume. Dance to it and invite your Team to join in and dance with you. Then, as always, thank your Spirit Guides for this fun, loving, and playful sign.

License Plate Signs

Our Spirit Guides can also use car license plates to get their messages across to us. License plates can be used for all sorts of messages and guidance that are relevant for your life at the time, or even at that particular moment. Some license plate messages are very straightforward and very obvious; you will be able to read the license plate and it will immediately mean something to you while with others you will need to be a bit more creative to understand the message. In my life, my spirit guides often use license plates as signs for their messages. Below are two examples of these signs that I want to share with you.

A few years ago I was parked outside a Petco store waiting for my husband Clayton. I was thinking about my beloved departed grandmother and how much I loved and missed her. A moment later a car arrived and parked in front of me. The car's license plate had the letters S-A-V-T- A. I did not know what the combination of those letters was meant to say in English; however, in Hebrew SAVTA means grandmother! You can imagine how blessed I felt and how thankful I was to my Spirit Guides and my savta, or grandmother, as well. To me that sign meant that my Spirit Guides were reassuring me that they understood my feelings, that they were there, and that my grandmother was very much alive and is with me.

Another wonderful sign I received through a license plate happened recently when I was driving on the freeway. That day, I greatly missed my younger sister living in Israel. A moment later, a car passed by me and some of the license plate had the letters I-R-I-T. The magical thing about it once again, is that my sister's name is Irit which of course is unusual in the United States. Yet my powerful Spirit Guides were somehow able to pull it off and show me the letters in order to validate for me that they were aware of the way I felt.

Two beautiful signs.

Signs Through Electronic Devices

Manipulation of electronic devices in our home is a sign that can be used by other members of our Team. Specifically, Spirit Guides and departed loved ones. For example, when a light bulb or a ceiling fan goes on and off, pay attention to what is on your mind or what is going on at that particular moment. If you are worried about your money situation, having a challenge with your children or your spouse, do not feel that well, or if you are happy, joyful and connected, know that the sign is simply meant to reassure you that your Spirit Guides are by your side, supporting you, aware of your feelings, guiding you, and are happy with you. Electronic signs most often are there to tell us that "We are right here. Everything is okay, and things are how they should be!"

Signs Through Conversations and Other People

When our Spirit Guides know specific information, a piece of advice, or a warning that we must receive, they will help us to be at "the right place at the right time" so that we can hear a partial conversation, a few sentences, or even just a few words spoken between other people that will convey their message to us. For example, I had a client who received a warning message from his Spirit Guides when he was out shopping. He was waiting in line to check out and, while he waited, there was a conversation between the two people in front of him. He heard one person telling the other about a fatal car accident that happened to his friend. "He always used to drive so fast I knew that one day it would happen to him", the man said. My client heard that and immediately related the story to himself and applied it to his reckless driving. He got scared and told himself "It must be a warning sign", which it was. From that day on my client had a pact with himself to slow down his driving and to never speed again. His Spirit Guide's sign had worked. In my client's reading his Spirit Guides validated that sign was a dire warning because they foresaw that, with the way he was driving, a tragedy was bound to happen. That sign saved his life.

A woman client came to see me and described the way her Spirit Guides related a message to her using other people's conversation. She told me that she was having a difficult time in her marriage. One evening, she was out for dinner and when she went to the ladies' room she happened to hear two women talking about their relationships and one of them gave advice to her friend. My client immediately related to that helpful advice and realized that she could use this stranger's advice in her own relationship.

In life, when our Spirit Guides are having a hard time getting through to us because we are consumed with thoughts and worries or are too stressed-out they will "use" other people who have the potential to influence us to deliver their messages. Here is an example of this. A mother is overwhelmed with the challenges that she is experiencing with her young child. Due to her overwhelmed mental state she is unable to recognize any of her Spirit Guides' signs of support. Unable to connect with her, her Guides will then show these signs to her close friends or family members so that they can point out these signs to her.

Fun Signs

Sometimes our Spirit Guides show us fun and playful signs that are very specific to us. For example, when we are ready to purchase a new car and are debating what make or model to get our Spirit Guides will navigate toward us the specific car and even the color that they know will suit us best or that they like. Try it out. When you are ready to buy a car, or are thinking about buying one, tell your Spirit Guides the kind of car you prefer and then ask them what they like most. Then, when you are out and about, pay attention and look around. They will navigate near you the exact car that they want you to see, not once or twice, but over and over again. You will start to see the same kind of car everywhere. The "car sign" is a playful sign, so have fun with it.

Another fun sign that our Spirit Guides enjoy showing us is pennies. However, because pennies are a sign that is also used by departed loved ones, I will be discussing this specific sign later in this chapter.

> **Work with your Spirit Guides' wisdom and creativity. Together you can communicate through signs.**

Signs from the Archangels and our Guardian Angels

Although some of the signs that are used by our Spirit Guides can also be used by the Angel members of our Team, such as specific songs, music, as well as using other people as messengers for their communication, there are some signs that are unique to them. Below I will list those signs and explain each one of their purposes.

Angels often use nature for their signs. Nature signs are one of their favorite ways to show us that they are nearby and that they love and protect us. Nature signs are also meant to soothe us and keep us calm as well as to strengthen our connection with them and with Gaia, our mother Earth. Please note that in general it is a very good idea to find time to interact with nature as much as possible in order to more easily sense, hear, and communicate with the Angel members of our Team and with Angels in general.

Sign: Hummingbirds and Butterflies

When you see a hummingbird flying near you or a butterfly landing on your body know that this is a sign from your Angels reassuring you that they are with you. When you see this hummingbird or butterfly do not think, doubt, or debate why they are there, but rather immediately acknowledge them as a sign from your Angels. When you see this sign, smile and be joyful. Then, just stay as still as possible, for as long as possible, so that you do not scare it off. Once they fly away, thank your Angels for the beautiful sign, feel their presence around you and express your love and gratitude to them.

Sign: Feathers

Feathers are obviously a sign that will leave no doubt to its meaning even with the most skeptical of people. Our Angels know that we human beings associate feathers with their appearance so this sign is a common sign that they like to use for not only a reassurance of their presence in our lives, but also for their existence in general. When you see a feather, usually white, sense how happy you become and how connected to your Angels you feel. Then, always pick the feather up and keep it in a special place. I have a small red box that I call my "signs' box". Over the years I have put all the signs that I have received from my Team members, including white feathers from my Angels, in it.

Sign: Rainbows

When the Angels use a rainbow, it represents protection. When you see a rainbow its a sign from your Angels that they are watching over you, protecting you, and are aware of your life on Earth. Rainbows also have a more significant meaning. It is a sign from our Creator that he, too, is protecting us and all other life forms as well as our planet. A rainbow is a magical sign that not only takes our breath away because of its immense beauty and mystical appearance, but also because it is such a major spiritual sign. The sign of a rainbow also helps our Angels provide us with encouragement for us to live our life to the fullest and to be grounded in the present moment. When our Angels give us the rainbow sign they also help us to feel grateful for who we are, for our lives, for the universe, and for them. Personally, each time I see a rainbow I have tears of joy in my eyes and feel connected to all of life and, of course, to God.

Sign: Scent

A beautiful sign that is often used by our Angels is the smell of roses or flowers. Our Angels use the sign of flower scents as a way to lift up our spirit when we have a difficult or challenging day. After all, who doesn't love a smell of fresh flowers? Angels also use this sign to, once again, express their love for us. By the way, Angels love roses of any kind or color. If you happen to have a garden, try your best to plant some roses of any kind or color. If you do not have the space to plant them, buy a bouquet of roses every once in a while and enjoy the bouquet. Once you are around roses their energy will act as a connector between you and your Angels and even attract additional Angels to your garden and home. Then try to make it a habit to "stop and smell the roses" alongside your Angels which I do every single morning on my way home from my meditation. The scent sign is more common than you think. As a matter of fact, once you are able to recognize the smell of flowers from your Angels you will be able to enjoy it on a daily basis, which of course, is wonderful.

Sign: Clouds

Angels are powerful beings that are able to shape energy in any form that they wish to and for any purpose. One of the ways in which they do that is by shaping a cloud in a specific way in order to communicate with us collectively, as well as, personally. Of course, in order to recognize the cloud sign you need to be creative and apply some wisdom to your interpretation of what the sign means. This means that it is obviously easy to understand a message from your Angels when you see a cloud in a shape of an Angel with wings which many people see; however it is not as easy to understand a cloud sign in a shape that is supposed to have a direct meaning personally to you or your life. For example, over the years I have heard people who were able to recognize a cloud sign from their Angels in a shape of a house when they needed validation for a move, or a "smiley-face" cloud that helped lift their spirits up on a difficult day, or a cloud in a shape of a dog or a cat for a specific message that they needed in regard to their pets. The cloud sign is a beautiful, fun, and playful way for your Angels to connect with you. Also, looking for the cloud sign will encourage you to look up at sky more often, which is always a very good thing.

Sign: Numbers

Another common sign that our Angels show us are combinations of numbers. Some examples of where you can see the number signs are in your car clock, your personal digital watch, an alarm clock, a computer clock, and in any public places that you happen to be, and so forth. There are various purposes for the numbers signs that we get from our Angels. Here are a few examples. When you happen to look at the clock and see the same numbers often, for example

3:33, 2:22, or 5:55, know that this is a sign from your Angels that are trying to reassure you that they are nearby and that you are not alone. When you see that number sign repeatedly acknowledge your Angels and express your love and gratitude to them. Seeing any combination of consecutive number such as 12:34, 3:45, or 4:56, a.m. or p.m., is a sign from your Angels that your life is going in the way it is supposed to. That sign also means that you are in the right place at the right time at the precise moment that you saw this sign. This sign does not always refer to some significant validation of a major event, experience, or decision in your life. Sometimes its simply there to reassure you that at this moment in time, whatever you are doing, you are okay, safe, and secure. I often see this number sign whenever I do something that I like such as enjoying a relaxing evening with my husband Clayton, having a pleasant dinner, or most commonly on Sundays, when we drive to town for a fun lunch we will see the time 12:34. Sometimes I see this number sign when I do chores that are not quite so pleasant, such as washing the dishes, cleaning the house, or doing laundry. I asked my Angels for the meaning of it and they told me that, even when I am doing the not-so-fun activities, I am in the right place at the right time and they are helping me accept this. The consecutive number sign always relaxes me and connects me with the present moment. A lot of people see the numbers 11:11 and ask me for the meaning. From what I have channeled over the years, this is a very important sign that has several important spiritual meanings. When you see the numbers 11:11, it is a message from your Angels telling you that your life is in balance and harmony or that you are ready to enter a more balanced life. This sign also signifies that you are growing and becoming more spiritually aware. The 11:11 sign is also a message from your Angels that they are pleased with where you are in this incarnation, so far, spiritually speaking. The most important meaning of the 11:11 sign is that at the time it is being shown to you, you are connected to all that is. You are one with your Angels, your Team, the universe, and with the Creator. The 11:11 number sign is a very blessed spiritual sign to be shown and so, when you see it, hold gratitude for your Angels as well as for your life.

An important note: There are, of course, many other number signs that our Angels show us in our daily lives. In order to recognize and understand them it is a good idea to educate yourself through reliable sources like books, workshops and research on the internet that discuss number signs from Angels and their meanings.

The Voice Sign: Calling Out Our Name

Sometimes the four Archangels as well as our Guardian Angels feel that they must get our attention urgently. Whether due to our stress level, mental state, a last minute warning, or when they realize that we are dangerously disconnected from their guidance, they will call out our name in a very loud and clear way. When this happens we will not hear our name coming from within us, meaning through an inner voice or intuitive feeling, but actually from outside of us as if another person were calling us. I remember the day that I first experienced this sign. It was right after the loss of my dear friend Richard. I was in the gym exercising on the elliptical machine. That day my grief was more than unbearable. I felt so deeply sad and lost over his passing. All of a sudden, I heard a male voice calling out my name. I looked around to see who was calling me and realized that no one was there. Being familiar with this sign, I asked who was it and was told that it was my Guardian Angel, Judah. I immediately understood his message. I knew that he was reassuring me that he was aware of my grief and that he, along with the other members of my Team, were supporting me in the grief process and that once again I was not alone. Needless to say, I felt much better and was immensely grateful for that magical sign that occurred just when I needed it most. The voice sign, although very clear, is not easily recognized by most people. Hearing their name being called out by an unseen entity can cause many people to become fearful, doubtful, and even go into denial and say something like, "I probably didn't hear that", or "I am sure that there is a perfectly logical explanation for it", or "The person that just called my name probably just left", etc. This sign more than most others requires our full spiritual openness and trust.

Signs From Our Departed Loved Ones:

From the Spirit World our loved ones keep in touch with us through various signs to tell us that they survived death, and to deliver messages of hope, guidance, and support. Many of the signs that we receive from our departed loved ones are also signs that the other members of our Team show us. A few of the signs are unique to them. The following are some examples of these.

Sign: Pennies, Dimes, and Other Coins

Pennies and dimes are a sign that is mostly shown to us by our departed loved ones; however, from time to time they are used as a sign from our Spirit Guides and Guardian Angels. When our departed loved ones show us a penny they will often try to put it in an unusual place. A place that we would never imagine for a penny to appear. They do this so that we will have no doubt that this is a sign. When you see a penny, you first and foremost must always pick it up and immediately acknowledge the fact that it is a sign. Then trust your intuition to tell you who it is that is showing it to you. Once you know which one of your departed loved ones gave you that sign trust your "knowingness" and thank your loved one for the sign. When you hold the penny in your hand, look and observe it carefully. Look at its shape, the year it was made, and what kind of penny it is because all these things could contain a hidden message. Once again, you must remain open-minded and creative to be able to recognize a message that is being given to you through the penny sign. For example, does the time that you found the penny mean something to your life? Does the location where you found it have any significance? How about the year on it? Did it have anything to do with your loved one's passing? And so forth. If you are unable to recognize a specific message or do not know why you received this sign or who gave it to you, simply enjoy the fact that any one of your departed loved ones is around, loving you, and communicating with you through this fun sign. With this specific sign, it is also important to remember that once you have seen the penny, picked it up and examined it, you need to separate it from "planet Earth money". Meaning, do not mix it with the change that you have in your wallet, purse, or change jar. Put the penny in your special place with your other signs. Over the years I have received a lot of pennies as signs from my loved ones in the Spirit World. A lot of them were from my beloved friend, Richard. As for Clayton, a few months ago he found an unusual looking silver, dime-sized medallion on the ground at the ATM. The front of it had a figure of a Guardian Angel. An obvious and beautiful sign. Sometimes I joke with my Team and ask them why they never show us quarters or dollar bills as signs in addition to the pennies. Their answer to that is, "For those you need to work". So pennies it is.

Sign: Phone, Emails, and Electronic Devices

Flickering light bulbs, microwave noises, and other electronic devices that are acting strangely are all signs that are shared with us by both our departed loved ones and our Spirit Guides. However, our loved ones in the Spirit World are often the ones who like to use our phones, both landlines and cellular, as a sign that they are around. Pay attention to a phone that is ringing and when you pick it up no one is there. Usually, if you happen to have a caller ID feature, it will say out of area. "Well, yeah", I'll say! Other times your phone will ring once or twice and then stop. Still other times, the phone will ring, you will pick it up, and there will be interference noises on the line. Another sign that is more specific to our loved ones in spirit is manipulation of a ceiling fan, or a stand-fan. Often the fan will be turned off and on or, when you have turned it off, and have left the room, when you return to the room it is back on. Over the years I often hear people discuss the fan sign. I had a client that lost her husband and, from the Spirit World, he would turn on the fan at night. My client was quite happy to know that her husband was around her and showing her a sign that he was alive and well. The problem was, however, that it was wintertime and that fan made the room too cold. So she asked me what to do. I told her to simply tell her husband that although she appreciated his efforts to show her a sign, it was much too cold and could he possibly use another sign and wait with the fan sign until the summer? It worked! This fun-loving soul stop turning on her bedroom fan and started to show her pennies. He also flicked on the living room lamp near the La-Z-Boy chair that he used to relax in when he watched television. By the way, my client contacted me a few months later and told me that her husband was, once again, messing with the fan, but he did wait till summer time. I wanted to include this story to remind you that signs from any of our Team members originate out of their immense love and great care for us. So, of course, they will take into consideration any request that we might have regarding a specific sign that they give us.

Although it is a more unusual sign, we might sometimes receive an unfamiliar email that will have the name of a person that has crossed over included in it. The name can appear either within the email address, the email subject, or the email content. I once received an email from a person named Richard. There was nothing else in that email, no message, no content, just the name. I immediately knew that, indeed, it was a sign from my friend, Richard, who said hi to me through that email. I thanked him for the sign and asked him for more emails from the Spirit World.

Sign: People Who Look Like Departed Loved Ones

Our loved ones in the Spirit World will sometimes manipulate or guide toward us a person that looks like they did when they were here with us, or that will clearly resemble the way they looked. This is a more unusual sign because it requires a great deal of effort for the soul to accomplish and it takes a long time for souls to learn how to do. A client told me that she was in a store one day and saw a man who looked exactly like her late husband. He had the same body shape, hair style and color, as well as similar facial features. The man looked like her husband when he was healthy, before he was sick. She stopped the person and told him that he reminded her of her husband who had died. I asked her what the man's reaction was. She said that not only he was very open and kind, but his energy, personality, as well as the way he spoke, was also similar to her husband. I told her how very blessed she was to have such a devoted husband in the Spirit World who was able to show her such a magical and powerful sign. I also commended her for her ability to recognize and trust the message of her husband's sign. Look around and pay close attention for people that look like or remind you of someone that you lost.

Sign: Dreams or Visits

Dreams, or visits as the Spirit World refers to them, are also considered to be a sign that our loved ones in spirit can use as a way of communicating with us. At night, when we enter a deep realm of sleep and the mind is finally inactive and free of thinking, the energy of our soul in the body or Higher Self, exits the body through the crown chakra at the top of the head, and travels into the Spirit World in order to re-charge its energy as well as interact and connect with our Team members and our departed loved ones. While our soul is out of the body, it is our Guardian Angels who watch over the body and ensure that the transitions of exiting and reentering the body are safely accomplished. I thought it was important for me to explain this process in a nutshell, so that you will be able to understand the extreme importance of sleep in our lives. Not only for the purpose of connecting to our loved ones in order to receive their messages and guidance through dreams, but, more importantly, to allow your soul to re-energize itself from the difficulty of being "stuck" in the physical body all day. Without giving our soul the opportunity to exit the body, even for a short period of time, you will feel exhausted, sluggish, and your energy will be low all day. Also, without a prolonged deep sleep, you will risk the chance of creating an illness in the body or a disorder of the mind.

Pay close attention to your dreams. If you remember a dream when you experienced a visit from a departed person, make it a habit to immediately write down everything that you can recall from the encounter. Where it was, the scenery, how your loved one looked, did they look young or old, what kind of clothes they wore, if you can recall any symbols that you saw, and what was being said or exchanged between the two of you. Try to remember if you received any messages or warnings. Learning how to interpret dreams can help you better understand your loved ones' messages as well as any other helpful guidance that dreams can provide. And so, I recommend that you look into dream interpretation books and other materials and make sure that you get the information from reliable sources.

Over the years people have told me that they have had a dream/visit from a departed person but that the dream was not pleasant and was actually scary, more like a nightmare if you will, and have asked me why this would have occurred. It is important to understand that when our soul is able to exit the body and interact with any of our Team members the experience is *always* pleasant, beautiful, and loving. The messages might be serious but the interaction will not, and therefore can not be scary. However, when the soul does not exit the body, and the dream is produced by the mind, then yes, a person can have a vivid and scary dream about the person that they have lost. Usually that sort of frightening dream, or nightmare, is the mind's interpretation of the passing, as well as, a reflection of grief. It can also be the expression of any unresolved anger that remains with the person who died, guilty feelings, and even the fear of one's own death. In general, when it comes to spirit communication during sleep, a *visit* is when our soul actually interacts with spirits, while a *dream* is when our mind is involved and creates or interprets the interaction.

Sign: Mutual Songs

Specific songs are a great sign that our loved ones in the Spirit World use to remind us of our life we had with them on Earth. Pay attention to the songs that immediately remind you of a person that you have lost, as well as how the song reminds you of them. Perhaps it is a song that you both enjoyed, danced to, listened to when you first met, or maybe it is simply a song that you know they loved, or that they knew that you loved. Romantic love songs are a sign from someone that we lost who we had an intimate relationship with on Earth. Perhaps someone that we dated, were married to, a life partner, and even a close friend that we dearly loved and cherished. Songs are a wonderful sign to receive from our departed loved ones and that create a powerful emotional response. When you hear a song and you know who is it from, acknowledge the sign and thank the soul. Then, get into a happy mood, sing to it out loud, dance, if it is possible, and visualize your loved one singing and dancing to that song along with you.

Sign: Smells

Although the Angel members of our Team can use various smells to make their presence known to us, certain smells that our loved ones in spirit use are different. Angels mostly use the scent of flowers and roses but a departed loved one will use very specific smells from life that will immediately remind us of them. Let me give you a few examples. It is very common for a grandfather to manipulate a cigar smell or the kind of cigarettes that they used to smoke on Earth. Mothers and Aunts will often manipulate a specific perfume that they used to enjoy. Fathers and husbands will use an aftershave smell or even a specific soap that they used to use after the shower. And, of course, any of these smell signs can also be used by any other soul of someone that we loved in life such as a friend or family member. The smell sign is a very magical and powerful sign to experience because you are actually able to physically smell the person that is now in the Spirit World.

Signs: At the Funeral and Memorial Service

Even when the soul of the person that we have very recently lost is unable to show us a sign yet due to the after-death process, it might, at the time of the funeral and or at the memorial, show their family and friends a sign. Many souls do, in fact, attend their own funeral and or memorial. Over the years I have heard about many different signs that were used by souls at the time of their funeral and memorial services. Here are a few of these signs. The most common sign that souls use at their funeral or memorial is "hugging" or wrapping their energy around their grieving loved ones and spreading their energy around the whole church or place of the service. People often describe how powerful and emotional this sign was as they were able to sense the energy of the person they lost around them and the place. They said that the energy was so strong and powerful that it left them no doubt that their loved one's soul was there with them attending the service. At their funeral, souls will also play with or manipulate one of their photos, the lights, the microphone, or the CD player if that is being used. They might also move the cover or tarp that is on the grave site, and again, even manipulate specific scents and smells that are specific to them, such as cigars, cigarettes, or perfume. Depending on the creativity, ability, and the awareness of the soul, even more specific signs can be used at the time of the funeral or memorial service. Try your best, despite the difficult and emotional time, to pay attention to anything that can help remind you of the person that you have lost and who is letting you know that they are there with you.

When it comes to signs from our loved ones in spirit it is important to understand that after the death of a loved one, it might take some time for us to receive signs from them. There are several reasons for this. Some of these reasons have to do with us, while others have to do with them. First, after death, signs from our loved ones are more difficult for us to recognize due to our grief. Grief is a normal process that every person goes through but can cloud the channel of communication, including sign communication with spirits in general, and with our loved ones more specifically. When grief is very heavy and it causes the person's mental and emotional states to become overwhelmingly distraught or, if the person has negative emotions like sadness, guilt, or anger over the passing, the chances of seeing a sign and recognizing its meaning is, unfortunately, very slim. As mentioned earlier, being able to recognize signs is dependent on our spiritual awareness and so when a person is closed-up with emotional distress the signs will be missed. The good news is that as time goes by and the person's grief lessens, their attitude becomes more positive, and if he or she grows spiritually the signs will become more easily recognizable.

In my work I often come across people who get upset, frustrated, and hurt when, despite their work on their personal grief, their high spiritual awareness, and openness to the concept of signs, they still have not received any signs from their loved ones after their passing. They often get nervous that the person who died might be angry at them, disappointed, upset, or simply have forgotten about them altogether. When it is a child who has died the parents may get scared that their child is trying to reach them but is lost somewhere or that their child does not know how to show them a sign because they were too young when they died. These are, of course, sad and false speculations of the mind. Before explaining to these people the reasons why they have not received any signs yet, I first reassure them that the person or child that they lost is an immortal soul now and so cannot ever be angry, upset, or disappointed with them regardless of the nature of the relationship that they had with them on Earth. Nor with the circumstances of their passing. Not receiving any signs from them does not mean they have forgotten about them or do not love them any longer.

There are a few spiritual reasons why some souls are unable to show their loved ones signs immediately after death. I will give a brief description of some of the reasons.

As discussed earlier, after death all souls go through various involuntary processes that help them enter the Spirit World and the amount of time it takes souls to complete these processes varies from soul to soul depending on different reasons. As long as a soul is still going through the process they will not be able to show their loved ones on Earth any signs until the process has been completed. For example, due to the amount of incarnations "under its belt" a more evolved and experienced soul will be able to complete the afterlife process much faster than the less evolved soul which will enable it to provide its loved ones on Earth signs much sooner. Depending on the time and the manner of death, sometimes souls will not be able to show their loved ones any signs because they are not near enough to planet Earth's dimension. For example, when a person dies prematurely in a horrendous death such as a suicide or a brutal murder, in order to clear up the negativity and pain that was accumulated prior to death, as well as the soul's need to recharge its depleted energy, the soul accompanied by its Spirit Guides and

115

other healing Light Beings will remove itself from planet Earth's dense vibration and travel to an energetically light, friendly, and pleasant planet or dimension. Sometimes, people may not receive any signs from the person that they have lost because their soul is simply not experienced enough with the ability to show them signs, especially signs that are more difficult to manipulate such as pennies or electronic devices. However, with the help of their Spirit Guides, they will eventually learn how to do it and communicate with their loved ones through signs. Sometimes you must simply be patient in order to receive signs.

> **In life, when you are able to recognize signs from any of the members of your Team it will not only strengthen your connection with them but will also make them very happy. So teaching yourself how to be aware of signs, as well as how to understand their meaning, is certainly worth the effort and adds to your spiritual growth.**

PART TWO

Practical - Making Contact

It this practical section of my book I will teach you the most effective ways to connect and communicate with your Team members. I will explain in detail the exact spiritual work that you must do in order to establish a successful connection and a clear channeling. Your job, of course, spiritually speaking, is to not only read the information but also to understand the concepts and apply the advice to your daily life, even the advice that I know might be difficult to practice. Then, you need to trust the process and remain patient until you achieve the results that you want.

Unfortunately, when people hear the amount of spiritual work that they need to do and the great amount of dedication that they need to have in order to successfully channel their Team, they often ask me if there are any "shortcuts" that can speed up the process. They also wonder why I do not simply teach them how to meditate and how to contact spirits without all the other work that is required. They might say, "It's through meditation that we essentially channel them... isn't it"? My initial reply to these questions is that, although in the beginning of my mediumship path I also wanted to find a short cut, I did all the difficult legwork and discovered that it did not exist. When it comes to channeling spirits there are no shortcuts that will take the place of hard and dedicated spiritual work that will shorten the path to successful channeling. This means that, no matter how successful your meditation sessions are and how good you are at sensing your Team and recognizing their signs, if you want to communication with them directly you must invest a great deal of spiritual work in your everyday life, throughout your entire life, and during every life. Otherwise, channeling your Team will never work. Remember that your Team are desperate to contact you directly, more than you can ever imagine! All you need to do first is to "want to want" to do it, and then, you need to do the necessarily spiritual work that is required to succeed. If I did it, so can you!

CHAPTER SIX

Communication Through Mind–Body-Spirit

When I started teaching people about the concept of the Team, I tried to find a way that would help them remember my teaching. I wanted to come up with a concept that would act as a daily checklist that they could use to help them remember the spiritual work they needed to do. I came up with the familiar phrase of "Mind-Body-Spirit" to help them review the work they needed to do each day on their mind, body, and their spirit.

Let me explain what I mean.

The Mind-Body-Spirit phrase has many different meanings that it brings to mind. In my teaching when I use the phrase Mind, I am referring to the negative aspect of our personality, our Ego. Body refers to our physical, mental, and emotional bodies. And Spirit refers to the Higher Self, the energy of our soul within our body. Connecting to our Team, whether it is through signs, the intuitive system, gut feelings, or direct communication, like inner voice, requires a disciplined mind/Ego, a nurtured and healthy physical, mental, and emotional body as well as an alignment with our spirit/soul. In life, when we work on disciplining our mind/Ego, nurturing and caring for the well-being of our physical, mental, and emotional body, we are able to align ourselves with the wisdom and power of our spirit/soul. Once we are balanced and aligned we can then open a clear channel to the Spirit World and to our Team. When we keep all three elements of our Mind-Body-Spirit properly aligned, balanced, and disciplined, will be able to more easily recognize and understand our Team's signs, listen to their guidance through our intuition and gut feelings, hear them through our inner voice, and even talk with them directly. On the other hand, if we do not, and we allow our negative Ego to govern our life and let our physical, mental, and emotional body become unhealthy and overwhelmed, we will be unable to align ourselves with our spirit/soul and will find it difficult, if not impossible, to achieve any sort of communication with any of our Team members.

In the next sections I will talk about each one of the elements of Mind-Body-Spirit as it relates to contacting your Team members. I will teach you about the Ego and how you can discipline it. I will talk about the spiritual and physical work that you will need to do for your physical, mental, and emotional body. And finally, I will explain how you can align yourself with your soul in order to use its great wisdom and power in your life. My hope is that once you understand the information I am providing you with you will be able to use the Mind-Body-Spirit checklist to assess your work and progress at maintaining their balance. For example, if at the end of a day you realize that although you were able to work on your body and mind, yet were unable to discipline your negative Ego, the following day you will need to put more effort on observing your mind and disciplining your Ego, in addition to maintaining your ongoing body/mind work.

> **The Mind-Body-Spirit checklist must be used daily until they are all balanced and healthy and a clear and open line of communication with your Team has been established.**

Disciplining the Mind

In this chapter I will provide you with detailed information and explanations of the Ego and how it can affect your connection and communication with your Team members. I will also teach you how to discipline your Ego, and how you can replace its negative power with the positive power of your soul. Also, because the Ego can stand in the way of our spiritual growth, which determines the degree of success or failure of the incarnation, I will describe ways in which you can move the Ego out of the way of your efforts to grow. This is a very important chapter. Try your best to apply the information and advice to your life and practice my lessons and guidance daily.

Ego is not just a concept; it is a real entity that has its own *energy field*. This is why in my teaching I refer to it as the *Ego Entity*. The Ego Entity consists of negative energy that is dense and heavy. Due to its negativity, the Ego Entity is harsh and not loving at all to say the least. A person's Ego Entity also loves drama of any kind, which is the fuel that keeps this entity alive. It does not matter to the Ego Entity what the drama is about as long as it is involved in it. The Ego Entity loves to experience and stir up life's dramas with whomever and about whatever. Anything that is considered drama, our Ego Entity loves. My own rule of thumb when it comes to my Ego entity and drama, is when I see drama about to occur I run the other way!

Some people's Ego Entity is stronger than other's meaning that they are more negative while others are willing to work on their Ego

Entity, and therefore become more positive. The more you work on ignoring your Ego Entity the more able you will be to lessen its strength. Regardless of the strength of a person's Ego Entity, all people have an Ego Entity because it is a necessary part of being a human. It is a part of our species' personality. As long as you are a human and of this planet, you will unfortunately have this negative entity within you. Over the years I have asked my Spirit Guides Lochem and B why God, with his immense wisdom and great love for us, created our mind with an Ego attached to it. Why do we have an Ego that at times can be so negative, destructive, and even dangerous to us, other people, and other species as well? Their answer was that we human beings are indeed a lazy species, spiritually speaking, and that we need a tough *opponent*. In our daily life, our opponent, the Ego Entity, forces us to change and grow spiritually by acting as a gauge that will help us measure the progress of our success in achieving that growth. It will also reflect back to us what we do not like within ourselves and will hopefully be able to change. My wise Spirit Guides continued on by explaining that if God had created human beings perfect, without an Ego, the whole concept of incarnating into this difficult planet for the sake of growth would be pointless, of course. Because if we were already created perfect, what is the point of growth?! If there is no growth we might as well remain in the Spirit World where we can achieve growth in much more pleasant ways. As you can see, the Ego Entity that we all have, although negative and destructive to every aspect of our lives, is very much necessary in our earthly incarnation as it has a direct effect on how much growth we are able to accumulate each lifetime. This is, of course, the measure of the incarnation's success. Here are two examples to help you better understand this concept. One of the many ways in which our Ego Entity can contribute to our soul's growth and evolution is through karma. In life, when our Ego influences us to act in negative ways that harms others, we create negative karma that taints our soul's energy field, which then stands in the way of its continued growth. The subsequent process of balancing that accumulated negativity contributes to our soul's overall growth and evolution. Negative temptations are another way in which our Ego Entity can force us to change, and therefore help our soul's growth. In life, when we come across a negative temptation in the form of another person or experience, our Ego will try to convince us to engage with that temptation and if we are able to choose to ignore it, we grow.

In an Earthly incarnation the energy field of the Ego Entity resides within our physical body and *shares* this space with another energy, the energy of our Higher Self, or our soul: the Creator's spark within us. And so in life, each one of us has two completely different energies that simultaneously reside within our body and can influence us in completely different ways. The Ego Entity within us can influence us to act and react in all kinds of negative ways. It causes us to distance ourselves from our fellow human beings. It acts as a separator. It causes us to become falsely fearful, to hate, to become jealous, envious, and to feel superior to others. It is because of the Ego Entity's negative influences that we are judgmental, enraged, angry, we lie, betray, and gossip, just to name a few of its negative influences. Also, due to the law of attraction of energies, the Ego Entity's negative energy attracts other negative energies toward us in the form of experiences as well as people who also have an equally negative Ego themselves which can explain the phrase, "Misery loves company". Once again, our Ego Entity is one of the main obstacles against any spiritual growth because when we are negative we are most likely not very spiritual. The good news is that the other energy that is within our body, the energy of our higher self, can also influence us. Our Higher Self, or our soul, acts as a connector between us and the world around us. It influences us to act in positive ways and inspires us to remain positive. It encourages us to understand others, to accept all people, to not judge, and, of course, to stay away from any drama. It is our Higher Self that encourages us to pursue our dreams and aspirations and to help others to do the same. Throughout our life our Higher Self also helps us to be fearless, to share, to accept, to give, to spiritually grow, and of course above all, to love. The energy of our Higher Self is calm, serene, neutral, joyful, and *one with everything.*

In life we each have a choice to make. We must decide which energy we want to follow, that of our Ego Entity or that of our Higher Self, or Soul. This is a daily choice and is crucial, not only for our spiritual growth, and therefore the success of the incarnation, but equally crucial to the degree of our connection with our Team and our ability to communicate with them. Next, I will explain the connection between our Ego Entity and our connection with our Team. When we allow our Ego Entity to influence us to engage in negative actions, the dense negative energy of those actions clouds up, and depending on the degree of negativity, even blocks the *tube/channel* that extends from the crown chakra and connects us with our Team. With a clouded or blocked channel any chance of a communication, direct or indirect, with any of our Team members will be impossible to achieve or to a lesser degree will be drastically reduced. A clouded or blocked channel will also cause us to become disconnected from them and therefore unable to receive their daily messages, guidance, and support. The degree to which we keep the channel clear that connects us to our Team and the Spirit World is what determines the strength and clarity of any communication that we wish to establish with any light entity that is "out of this world"!

In order to establish and maintain a clear and open communication channel we must discipline our Ego Entity and not let it influence us. The way we do this is by making choices that will help us *side* with the energy of our Higher Self and not with the energy of our Ego Entity. This means that every minute of every day throughout our life, and every life, we need to make choices and decisions that are *energetically compatible* with the energy of our Higher Self and not with the energy of our Ego entity. This is done with positive choices and actions, not negative ones. The way we do this is by becoming alert, focused, and conscious of each and every one of our daily choices. Each time that we are ready to react, interact, think, decide or make a specific choice of any kind, we must always choose correctly and side with our soul. Basically, when we identify that our Ego Entity wants us to do A, then we must do B. Here are a couple of examples of what I mean. Someone cuts you off on the freeway. Your Ego Entity needs an immediate "anger fix" and tries to influence you to become hateful. To yell and swear at the other driver, or worse, act out in a road-rage manner. Well don't. Just before you are ready to react, count to ten, which, by the way, is a spiritual concept, and use those few seconds to connect to your soul which will help you to remain relaxed and calm. Put your favorite radio station on and continue driving in peace. In another example, imagine that a friend comes to you with gossipy news about a mutual friend. Your Ego Entity needs a "superiority fix" and wants you to do A, which is to engage in the gossip and perhaps even add a few more juicy details of your own. Once again, just before you are ready to allow your Ego Entity to influence you, stop! Count to ten, and then do B, which is to tell your friend that you are uncomfortable engaging in any negative discussion about your mutual friend and let it go. Change the subject altogether and talk about something else immediately. Try to apply these two above examples to any other scenario in your life where you need to replace an immediate negative reaction from your Ego Entity with a positive one that is inspired by your soul.

In life, when we make a clear and firm decision to side with our Higher Self, we take the power away from our Ego Entity, and therefore weaken it. The more we do it, the weaker it gets. It is also important to examine how, technically speaking, this happens. First, at the precise moment when we choose to ignore the negative influence of our Ego Entity, we side with our soul and shine its light on the Ego's negative energy, literally speaking. It is that powerful light that weakens it. Then, over time, the more light we shine on its dark nature, the less powerful it gets. However, the spiritual work that it takes to side with our soul and not our Ego Entity, meaning switching from negative choices to positive ones, will take a lot of dedication and consistency and, most of all, patience. Deciding to side with your soul must be practiced over and over, again and again, day after day, minute by minute, until your life is free, or mostly free of the negative influences of your Ego Entity. Once you are free, your soul will govern your life, which will reassure you with a more pleasant, calm, and positive life, as well as a clear and open communication channel to your Team members. Be prepared, however, your Ego Entity, which has its own intelligence, will immediately detect your intention to "kill it" and with its arrogant attitude and need to remain alive, it will most certainly fight hard for its survival. The good news is that each time you ignore it and side with your soul, you stand up to its illusionary power and win. Once you have started to work on disciplining your Ego Entity, some days will be better than others. During the not so good days when you feel that you are "falling off the wagon" your Ego Entity will take center stage and be in full control. This will make you feel that you are unable to stop its negative influence and observe yourself being sucked into it. On these days when your Ego is governing your day, you will be negative, you will look for fights, and you will seek drama. You might be angry, judgmental, or become jealous, and it will certainly be more difficult for you to express love, even to the people that you care for the most. When you experience these days, try not to be too hard on yourself. Especially if you have been trying to discipline your Ego Entity for some time. Tell yourself that it is okay to still be under its influence because after all, it gathered its power and strength and was in full control for many, many years. Naturally, it will take some time to weaken it. Remind yourself that all spiritual work takes time and that any major change, especially spiritual change, does not happen overnight. Most of all try to remain patient until you get back on the wagon again, so to speak. On the other hand, during the good days, the days that your Ego Entity is weak and disciplined, you will feel connected and aligned with your soul which will enable you to remain positive, joyful, calm, serene, neutral, and in control, spiritually speaking. During these good days, your communication channel with your Team will be clear and open which will help you to sense them and recognize their signs and understand their meanings. Your intuition system will also function effectively and your sixth sense will be sharp. You will even be able to hear your Team members and communicate with them directly. When you experience these fantastically good spiritual days, when your Ego Entity is dormant and weak due to your dedicated daily spiritual work, be proud of yourself and of the progress you have accomplished. Be grateful for the results that your hard work has produced.

When people remain negative for a long time, their Ego Entity will gather more and more strength until it runs wild and completely governs their entire life. A negative, out of control wild Ego Entity that is left undisciplined for many years will eventually alter a person's behavior and personality to the point where it will be difficult to even recognize the person. A person that we deeply love for example, who has an undisciplined Ego Entity for many years, will start acting like a stranger, someone that we do not even know anymore or a creature from another planet. This is sad but true. In extreme cases, a person with a powerful Ego Entity that was left unchecked for too many years can become dangerous to themselves and to society. Serial killers and pedophiles have this kind of a dangerous Ego Entity that causes them to not even act human anymore. Their eyes look energetically dark and empty and the way they look and act is more like a demon than a person. The "Night Stalker" serial killer, Richard Ramirez, during the early Eighties in Southern California, is one example of that sort of Ego Entity gone wild and then deadly. Of course you can imagine that these dangerous people's channel to the Spirit World is completely blocked which causes them to become utterly disconnected from their soul, from their Team, and from God. This, of course, explains their heinous acts. Unfortunately nowadays, although to a lesser degree than the above example, most people find it easier to side with the energy of their Ego Entity rather than doing the necessary spiritual work that it takes to side with their soul. Because of the nature of energy, both positive and negative, it can never stay the same. This means that it either grows in power or weakens. Those who allow their Ego Entity to grow in power and become out of control in their *personal* lives will also contribute to the *collective* Ego Entities of humanity as a whole. This concept can easily be recognized in the state of our world, we have conflicts between countries, different religions, political groups, neighbors, and among family members. Many leaders who are supposed to protect, guard, and guide us, more often mislead and lie to us. Too many people tend to hate, judge, disrespect, negatively use and become cruel to one another as well as to other species. A majority of people also do not respect Gaia, our Mother Earth, nature, or our beautiful planet. That behavior and disrespect angers Gaia, our Mother Earth, who in return retaliates with ever increasing natural disasters and other tragedies. And so it is obvious, that many human beings are disconnected from their souls and are governed by the wrong energy, that of our collective Ego Entity, because if the collective energy of our Higher Selves were to govern, we would have been living in a completely different world than the one we do now. So obviously we must change. And that change must first start with us and with the positive choices that are in line with our souls that we must make in our daily lives. Because positive energy can also grow in power in the same way that negative energy does, and because we are all connected and are all one, the energy of these positive choices will spread out into our world and will tip the scale of our collective energy from negative to positive. That is when our planet will once again thrive.

> **By disciplining your Ego Entity and siding with the beautiful energy of your soul, you will enjoy Heaven on Earth alongside your Team.**

Balancing the Body

The well-being of our physical, emotional, and mental body has a direct effect on our connection to our Team members and to the spirit world. In this section I will talk about how and why our food, sleep, exercise, clothes, and the activities that we engage in can all influence not only how we feel physically and mentally, but also how it affects our energy, spiritual awareness, and connection to our Team.

On Earth, our body is the vehicle in which our soul drives around. It is where part of our soul energy resides for the length of each incarnation. In life there are the obvious reasons why we must take care of our physical, emotional, and mental body but there are also just as important spiritual reasons for us to do that. We must care for the well-being of our body and state of mind so that we can stay healthy, avoid future illnesses, or die before our pre-designed time.

How healthy we are physically and mentally will determine the quality of the life that we have. The better we feel, the more comfortable we get and the happier we become. Taking care of ourselves also ensures that we will be able to stay here on this planet for whatever amount of years that our soul pre-designed for us. Because, after all, our soul needs its suit, the body, to remain on this planet. The spiritual reasons why we must care for the body involve the energy, or the Chi, that "feeds" our body and gives it life. In the body we have seven main chakras which are doorways or passages through which the energy enters and exits our body. When the body and mind of a person is healthy, well-nourished, and balanced, the Chi within the body will flow at a vibrant and lively speed. At a vibrant speed the Chi will help the body and the brain to remain strong and healthy. The immune system will be fully functional and doing its job of protecting the body from any invaders. The brain will produce all the right chemicals, the cells will divide in an orderly manner, and all the body systems and organs will do what they are supposed to do. With that kind of a healthy body we will not only feel healthy and energetic in our body and mind, but we will also be able to clear up and open the communication channel that connects us to our Team, assuming of course that we do all of the other necessary spiritual work like meditation, disciplining the Ego, etc.

On the other hand an unhealthy, unbalanced, neglected, or abused body and mind will interfere with the natural flow of Chi within the body. With the body in this state, the Chi will, of course, still enter our body through the various chakras, but will flow at a slow and sluggish speed. With the slow moving energy the body will not be able to heal itself from illnesses or symptoms, the immune system will be compromised and will not be able to fully protect the body from present or future illnesses, and with a slow Chi the body might even create new illnesses, symptoms, or disorders. The mind which will also suffer from a lack of energy flow will cause our mental state to become fragile and weak, meaning that we will have a harder time handling our life's challenges and problems. We will also become dis-proportionally emotional, aggravated, distraught, and frequently overstressed. With a body and mind that is only partially functional, we will experience very low energy all day, every day no matter how much we sleep or rest. The body will also create weird and unusual symptoms and discomfort in various areas of the body and life will obviously not be super joyful for us, to say the least. Most importantly, an unhealthy body and a sluggish Chi within it will cause us to become "heavy" energetically speaking, which will cloud up and even block the channel altogether depending on how bad of shape we are in. With a low and heavy energy, we will most likely be unable to recognize or be aware of any messages that our Team members are showing us through our intuitive feelings, gut feelings, signs, inner voice, as well as any other direct communication. So it is crucial that we take care of ourselves.

Food

There are two types of food that can influence the well-being of our body. The first one includes natural food products such as fruit, vegetables, healthy grains, nuts, any quality source of vegetable protein, and water, of course. This group of foods is considered to be alkaline food and has various nutrients and pH qualities that are helpful to the body's digestive system and its functioning in general. This group of foods is also considered to be light in energy which will help the Chi within the body flow smoothly and facilitate the communication channel to our Team to stay clear and open. The other group of food includes red meat, carbohydrates, sugars, gluten products, salt, and packaged foods that contain too much sodium, caffeine, and alcoholic beverages which all have ingredients that go against the function of the body making it difficult for the digestive system to break them down. Today, some of the products in this group of foods are harmful to our body due to the unhealthy preservatives that food manufacturers use which can decrease the ability of the body to function and even damage it outright. Energetically speaking this group of foods has a heavy energy that affects the natural flow of the Chi in the body which will then cloud up or block the communication channel. It is important to make sure that you base the majority of your diet on natural, alkaline foods because it has a direct effect not only on the way your body will function, and therefore on the way you feel, but also on your ability to connect to your Team members.

In my work over the years I have noticed how much more effective my communication with the Spirit World became once I began eating natural and alkaline food. Eating alkaline food in small portions throughout the day, in addition to drinking a lot of water keeps me energetically light and keeps my communication channel to the Spirit World clear and wide open. Keeping a healthy nutritional diet, daily exercise routine, and plenty of water, not only makes me feel more vibrant and energetic, but the messages that I channel from my Team members as well as other spirits are much clearer and easier to receive and understand. Having said that, however, I believe that food can be so much fun and in this harsh planet we certainly can use some more fun. Food, even in the not-so-healthy group, can certainly be delicious. Also, how great and fun is it to dine out, entertain friends for a dinner party, or cook together with a loved one in the kitchen? And so balance, which is of course a spiritual concept, is the key in this case. For myself, although I am strict with what I feed my body, I did not and will not give up some of the "heavy" foods that I love so much, especially pizza. It seems that for me the best way to get the best of both worlds is to stay strict with my food intake Monday through Saturday, and on Sundays I give myself a break and eat "less spiritual" food and enjoy it.

I also want to talk briefly about red meat as I frequently have people who are confused by my including it in the "not healthy" food group. Obviously, a lot of people insist that red meat has a source of protein that is healthy and even necessary for our body and, to some degree, they are right. However, from a *spiritual perspective*, especially in our world today, red meat is considered heavy food energetically speaking due to the way most factories and CAFOs treat the animals and the unfortunate cruelty that is inflicted on them. And so, if you insist that red meat is good for you, perhaps you can take my spiritual advice into consideration and minimize your intake. As for myself, for over twenty years I have not consumed any red meat or any other meat for that matter because of the spiritual aspect of it as well as for the consideration of animals' rights.

Water

Water also greatly affects us. Drinking plenty of water can obviously help the functioning of our physical body. But drinking plenty of water and hydrating the body also has a spiritual benefit that is important to understand. The Chi within our body and water are energetically connected with one another which is why spirits often refer to water as "spiritual medicine". When we drink plenty of water we create a "silky-like" environment in the body that helps the Chi flow more smoothly. On the other hand, when we do not drink enough water, we create in the body a dry and rough environment that makes it harder for the Chi to flow. The amount of water that we drink can, and will, influence how smoothly the Chi within us will flows which will then affect every aspect of our well-being physically, mentally, emotionally, and certainly spiritually.

Exercise

We all know the importance of exercise and the great benefit that it has for the well-being of our body and mind. But we must also understand that exercise has a direct effect on our spiritual awareness, the connection to our Team, and to the Spirit World in general. I have rarely heard spirits refer to exercise as "exercise"; they usually use the phrase "moving the body". When I ask the reason for this they told me that in our world when people use or hear the word *exercise* they mostly refer to weight-loss and muscle-building (which of course will happen anyway as a byproduct of exercise). However, the phrase "moving the body", refers more specifically to the spiritual benefits that exercise provides us with. The following are some of these spiritual benefits. When we move the body, especially when we engage in cardiovascular exercises, we positively affect the Chi energy. When we exercise we "speed up" the Chi that enters the body and help it flow smoothly within the body. Exercise also helps the chakras spin more effectively and smoothly which then helps clear any negative residue that is clouding or blocking the doorways where the energy enters various areas of the body. And finally, because exercise produces endorphins in the brain, we become energetically "lighter" which then positively affects our mental state. Unfortunately for most people, exercise is more than a bit of a hassle. It takes time and effort and, for the most part, it is not enjoyable. I find, however, that once people, including myself, understand the importance of exercise from a spiritual perspective, in addition to the benefit of a healthy body, mind, and weight loss they tend to look at it differently which then helps them to be committed to a daily exercise routine. It is important for me to note here that in order for you to enjoy the spiritual benefits of exercise you do not need to run for miles and miles nor do you need to exercise for hours at a time. All you need is a good-paced cardio exercise that will raise up your heart rate four to five times per week and, of course, a consistent routine. For my own exercise routine, I jog on my treadmill for thirty minutes and walk uphill for five. I then do twenty minutes of weight training. I do this routine Monday through Friday in the early morning and on Saturday and Sundays I allow my body to rest and enjoy this time in bed. Once again, balance is the key.

Sleep

It is obvious that by giving ourselves plenty of sleep we allow our physical body the opportunity to recharge and heal itself. In addition to that, from a spiritual perspective, sleep or the lack of it has a direct effect on our ability to connect and communicate with our Team. When we have a good night's sleep we feel well-rested and refreshed in the morning. Our energy, as well as our mental state, is uplifted which puts us in a better mood. With an uplifted mental state and a happy attitude we are able to more easily do the necessary daily spiritual work that connects us to our Team. Not being tired can also help us stay more focused on our surroundings, and therefore recognize any of our Team members' messages that they show us through different signs or through our intuitive system, for example. Being fully rested also enables us to meditate more effectively which can give us the opportunity to directly communicate with them. From a spiritual perspective, sleep is also very important to the part of our soul that incarnated into this life, our Higher Self. As mentioned earlier, at night once we enter the deep sleep state and our mind is completely inactive, the energy of our Higher Self exits the physical body through the crown chakra at the top of the head and travels to the Spirit World in order to recharge its energy and interact with our Team and other spirits. Once our Higher Self is out of the body, our powerful Guardian Angels are the ones who ensure the safety of this fascinating process including the exiting of the Higher Self from the body, the entering of the Spirit World, and, of course, the returning to the body.

In readings, spirits frequently express to people the great importance of quality sleep and often provide helpful tips on how to achieve it. These tips have helped me greatly over the years as well. I have listed some of them here. Establish good sleeping habits. Try to go to bed at the same time each day, not too late and not too early. Nine p.m., or so, seems to work well for me. Have a pleasant bed and a clutter-free bedroom environment. Nice clean sheets, pleasant smells, and so forth. Do not exercise too late in the day. And of course, do not engage in any negativity or drama of any kind throughout the day and more specifically before getting ready to go to bed. If your mind is overly active when you go to bed there are a lot of helpful techniques that can assist you to quiet your thinking. Some of these include visualization of pleasant things or scenes. Such visualizations include natural ones like the ocean, forest, snow, or desert, visualizing your pets, your loved ones, both in life and in spirit, Angels with white soft wings, or any of your other Team members. You can also visualize the white light, or the Chi entering your physical body and spreading around all your organs, especially your heart, which, by the way, is also helpful for strengthening your immune system. You can use soft, quiet music that is soothing and pleasant. There are also many other therapeutic relaxation techniques that you can research, such as specific forms of meditation and various additional tools that you can use to help you relax. Basically, find what works best for you. You can also ask your beloved Team members to help you get a good night's sleep. Ask them to soothe you and to calm your energy down so that you can relax and fall asleep more easily. Ask them to ease your mind from over thinking and worrying. Always keep in mind that the most basic thing that can help soothe and relax you, resides within you. It is your Higher Self, your serene and calm soul, of course. You simply need to develop a way to connect and align yourself with it. If you feel, however, that you have tried all these spiritual tips and still find it difficult to relax and fall asleep and want to use any kind of external remedies, stick with anything that is *natural*. When it comes to sleep aids it is best to stick with herbal and naturopathic medicines that will work with your body and mind to help you rest. Try your best to stay away from sleeping pills or any other western medicine, i.e. pharmaceuticals, as they are only a "band-aid" that covers up the problem of your inability to relax and literally "drugs" you to sleep.

The Clothes We Wear

The type of clothes that we wear, both the fabric as well as the colors, can have an effect on our well-being, our mental state, and our mood which obviously can greatly affect our ability to contact our Team and receive their communication.

Every fabric of clothing has its own energy. Natural fabrics such as linen, hemp, cotton, silk, and wool have a "friendly and light" energy that affects not only our mental state and mood but also the

Chi in our body in the same way that alkaline foods and water do. It allows it to flow smoothly and efficiently, and therefore, the body functions more effectively. On the other hand, unnatural fabrics such as polyester, nylon, acrylic, and spandex have a more "heavy" energy which can affect our mood and cause us to become sluggish. So when you choose your clothes be picky about the fabric. Try your best to stick with natural fabrics as much as possible and stay away from any man-made ones. The color of our clothes can also have an effect on us which is why it is important to use colors that are soft and natural such as white, blue (any shade), tan or khaki, purple (any shade), green (any shade), and yellow, like the color of the sun. I refer to those colors as *"reflectors"* because they are able to reflect energy away from us which can be helpful when we are around any negative energy. On the other hand, I refer to red (any shade), orange (any shade), gray, or black as *"absorber"* colors. When we wear these colors they absorb any energy that is around us instead of reflecting it away from us which can be harmful when negative energy is around. By the way, despite the common belief, black is not the color of evil, but rather a color that absorbs the most energy of all the colors which is why it should only be worn occasionally. It is a good idea to avoid wearing any of the absorber colors when you know that you are going to come across any negative energy in the form of a person or an experience because wearing an absorber color will not only absorb that negative energy but also put you at risk of getting "stuck" with it. Also, if you have an occupation were you directly interact with a lot of different people, such as an energy healer, massage therapist, therapist, nurse, doctor, or in retail, for example, it is much better if you choose to wear clothes with reflector colors as well as clothes that are energetically friendly in their fabric.

When reading the information about the fabric and color of our clothes that we wear, we must once again keep in mind the spiritual concept of balance. Although some fabrics and colors are indeed more energetically friendly than others and can affect us in different ways, it does not mean that you should not purchase an outfit that you like that is red or black and has a fabric that is not natural, or get rid of clothes that you have in your closet that have an unfriendly fabric. The information I have provided you with is merely intended to help you be knowledgeable so you are aware of what and how the clothes that you wear affect you energetically, mentally, and spiritually.

Playfulness

Playfulness is a spiritual phrase that refers to activities that are compatible with the fun-loving energy of our soul. These are activities that our soul loves. On our planet, playfulness is *a necessity not a luxury*! This means that we must engage in playful activities despite our hectic life, lack of time, challenges, or any other excuse, legitimate or not, that we might give ourselves in order to avoid allowing ourselves to be playful. Some of these activities include interacting with Gaia, Mother Earth, by spending time in nature, such as enjoying the beach or going camping, listening to music, dancing, or hobbies that bring you joy such as painting, writing, cooking, creating something with your hands, going out to dinner and spending time with close friends and family members, who, of course, are not draining and do not seek drama, engaging in any activity that makes you laugh, such as a comedy show or a funny movie, exercise outside like hiking or swimming in the ocean or a lake, hugging and kissing your loved ones often, and relaxing like taking a nap, reading a book, or watching television. When it come to television try to be picky as to the type of programs that you watch as well as limiting the amount of time.

Because it is difficult for the energy of our Higher Self to be trapped in the dense physical body for year after year, engaging in any of these above-mentioned activities will give our soul the opportunity to come out and play which will then cause us to be joyful, happy, and in peace. Engaging in playful activities will also improve our mental state, our mood, and the well-being of our body. With a happy mind and body we can stay open, spiritually speaking, to receive and recognize signs and messages from our Team. When we play and have fun, our Team members, being playful themselves, will certainly join us which will strengthen our connection we have with each one of them. In life, however, not every activity that you, or rather your Ego, might consider to be fun is a playful, spiritual activity that will help you connect with your soul energy. For example, going camping with some fun-loving, close friends in order to enjoy nature and some fun times is certainly a spiritual activity that your soul will love. Going camping with some friends for the sake of drinking and getting hammered, is not! And so when you plan to have fun, think carefully if the activity that you are going to engage in, as well as the people that will accompany you, are compatible with the beautiful energy of your soul which will reflect in a playful activity. Or, if the activity is influenced by your negative Ego Entity which most likely reflects stupidity. It only requires a little common sense to differentiate between the two.

Friends

The friends that we keep in life also have a direct connection to our physical and emotional well-being. From a spiritual perspective, the wrong friends, a negative friend that is, can and will cause us to become stuck in our effort to spiritually grow which will naturally interfere with our connection to our Team.

Throughout life, when we are young, middle-aged, or older, the friends that we have, specifically the ones that are considered to be our "soul mates" and with whom we have a soul contract, play a significant role in the incarnation and so each significant friend that we have is there for the reason of providing our soul with a variety of growth opportunities. However, because we are not robots but living, active beings, not all the friends that we have are souls with whom we are supposed to share certain experiences with for the sake of growth. Sometimes it is our negative Ego Entity that influences us to choose certain friends that are not good for us, to say the least. Friends that are negative in nature, energetically draining, drama seeking, have bad habits, such as heavy drinking, drug abuse, or friends that have a reckless personality, or are engaged in dangerous behaviors. When we let these kinds of people into our life and allow them to influence us we take the risk of shifting away from our soul plan, our spiritual path, as well as from our Team. Because if we drink and do drugs with one friend, gossip, fight, and engage in heavy drama with another, for example, our own energy will be compromised and drained which will make it impossible to have the energy that is required for the daily spiritual work that we need to do in order to grow in awareness and communicate with our Team. With the lack of spiritual work, the Higher Self within the body will be pushed aside leaving the Ego Entity totally in control which, of course, is always bad news. Draining and negative friends can also reflect their own negativity onto us and change our mood and mental state. Besides, with the wrong friends you might find yourself ending a foolish and reckless night on the town in jail, or worse yet in a grave instead of in the warmth of your comfortable bed.

It is important to understand that the kind of friends that we choose to have in life are also very important to our Team. When they foresee that we are ready to befriend a person that is not good for us, they will do all that they can to influence us to change our mind by bringing to our attention some obvious indications that we are not a good fit for friendship. However, once again, the final decision is left for us to make. This is why it is important to be picky with your friends, the ones that you have now and any new ones that will enter your life in the future. Guard yourself from any friends who do not mirror the best intentions that you have for yourself, for your spiritual path on Earth, and for the overall plan of your soul.

It is also important to understand that in life, when we spiritually grow and change, so do our friends. In my work I often come across people who get their feelings hurt when their childhood friends are not in touch with them anymore while other people complain that all of a sudden they realize that they do not have much in common anymore with a friend that they knew for a long time. I explain to these people that it is normal for us to change our friends in the course of our life and it is actually something that our soul *prefers* as it teaches us different lessons and provides us with different growth opportunities at various stages in our life. Also, it is obvious that when we are in our mid-twenties, for example, we will naturally attract and interact with completely different sets of friends than when we are in our mid-forties or sixties. Do not be sad or upset then if a friend stops contacting you or if you are in a place in your life where you are changing some of your friends. Understand it from a spiritual perspective and wish all your previous friends the best in their future. Then open yourself up to new friends. Ones who will mirror your present spiritual awareness, energy, as well as your activities.

Carefully review all the friends in your life. If you know that you have a friend that continues to be negative, draining, constantly seeking drama, or lacks any sort of spiritual awareness, you should of course remain kind but ultimately try to limit your time together or end the friendship altogether.

> **Balancing the body has many different aspects. How dedicated you are to working on each and every one of these aspects will determine how well-tuned and functional the vehicle is in which your soul "drives" while you are on this planet.**

Using the Spirit

In life, when we do the necessary spiritual work, we move the Ego Entity out of the way and establish a strong and healthy body and mind. Then as a healthy, balanced, and Ego-less human being we build a solid spiritual awareness that enables us to become aligned with the energy of our soul in our body, our Higher Self. Of course as spiritual people, our connection to our Team as well as our ability to communicate with them will also increase in clarity and strength each day.

Aligning ourselves with our souls provides us full access to the immense wisdom and great spiritual power that we inherit from the Creator and can then use in our daily life. Aligning with our soul also helps us to regain the memory that we lost at the time of birth. The full knowledge of who we truly are beyond this world. We will recall that our name, sex, race, what we do for a living, our family status, our personality, what we have achieved and have not achieved, and all of our successes and failures are a small part of who and what we are *in this life only.* And that this life, as well as all of the past and future lives, are only parts of the bigger picture of our existence as souls. On Earth, gaining this enlightened realization of our true nature will help us to detach and de-identify from our mind and from our life experiences, both the good and the difficult ones. Then, once detached we will be able to have more of a neutral attitude toward the outcome of our life experiences, the same way our soul does. Recalling who we are beyond this world is considered to be one of the greatest spiritual achievements in any given incarnation on Earth. An achievement that will benefit not only our life here on this planet, but also our soul's overall growth and evolution.

Authentically understanding that the life that we now live contributes to the bigger plan of our existence as souls will also help us to live life to the fullest, enjoy each and every moment of it, and value all the experiences and people as they are all potential growth opportunities for our soul.

Once we are able to become aligned with our soul, the life that we used to have, which was mostly governed by our Ego Entity, will be left behind and be replaced by a beautiful new form of existence. An existence that will be governed by the beautiful nature of our soul. With a soul-governed existence, life will be less fearful, less negative, and not as lonely or chaotic because our soul is fearless, powerful, joyful, positive, serene, and one with all that is. Obviously, however, as long as we still live here on this harsh and dense planet, with our complex mind and body, and among other human beings, life will continue to present us with various challenges and experiences that might bruise us and cause us some aches and pains but with a strong connection to our powerful Team and the inspiration of our wise soul we will be able to look at these challenges and experiences from a much different perspective. We will be able to more clearly and effectively examine them in order to understand and discover why they are there, what it is they are supposed to teach us, and how our soul is supposed to grow from them. And believe or not, one day, we will come to the realization that all our difficulties and problems are actually blessings in disguise.

In summary, when we are aligned with our soul as well as with our Team, we become more loving, understanding, and less judgmental human beings. We will also exhibit more compassion toward other people, the ones that we know, as well as complete strangers. Planet Earth in all its forms will also be in our top priority. We will teach people about the importance of peace rather than war, truth rather than lies, and spirituality over the rigid rules of religion. Connecting to our soul and our Team members will also inspire us to value all life and become one with all that is. Valuing all life forms will naturally connect us to nature, to animals, to all living beings, and to God as the creator of all of them. Then, governed by our soul and powered by our Team, we will spread the love of the creator into this world one person at a time, one day at a time, until a complete, positive, spiritual shift occurs.

> **By becoming aligned with our soul and using it to better our life, the lives of others, and our world, we will be transformed into an enlightened, spiritual human being. And as such, we are obligated to try to help others to become transformed themselves. We must, however, follow the most important rule of a teacher which is that we must always practice what we preach!**

CHAPTER SEVEN

Meditation

Due to the importance of this topic I will divide this chapter into three separate sections. First, I will give a general description of meditation. Next, I will provide you with some helpful tips and tricks to help you achieve more effective meditation sessions. Finally, I will teach you how to quiet your mind so that you can connect to your Team. My hope is that by understanding the concepts of meditation, following my tips and tricks, and effectively shutting off your mind from thinking you will build a strong foundation for clear and effective communication with any of your Team members, as well as elevating your spiritual awareness and improving the quality of your life in general.

General Information

Meditation refers to the ability to quiet the mind from thinking. When we meditate we ascend to a higher level of consciousness enabling us to connect with a higher spiritual power and wisdom, the power and wisdom of our Higher Self, our soul, our Team members, our departed loved ones, and other spirits. Meditation also has a direct effect on our well-being, physically, mentally, and certainly spiritually. The first and foremost benefit of meditation is that we can spend some time alone with the one person that we need to take care of the most, ourselves!

Because meditation is the foundation of all spiritual growth it must be included in our daily life if we value our spiritual awareness in general and, specifically, our connection to our Team. I am often asked if one can become spiritual without meditating. The answer to that question is yes, of course they can. If you work on defeating your Ego Entity, care for the well-being of your body and mind, and allow your soul to govern your life you will indeed become an enlightened spiritual human being. Meditation, however, has many other spiritual benefits that will lift a person even higher spiritually speaking to a level that they will not be able to reach without it. Besides, once you invest the great amount of time and effort in your spiritual growth through balancing your mind-body-spirit, *not* meditating doesn't make sense because meditation will improve the daily work that you already do. Basically, meditation is an inseparable part of any spiritual work and without it that work is not fully complete.

There are many different techniques for meditation. Because people are different and have different levels of experience with meditation, some techniques might work for one person and not for another. This is why it is a good idea to try a few different meditation techniques and see which works best for you. For example, at the beginning of my spiritual path when I was new to meditation I found that guided meditation made it easier for me to quiet my mind. In my guided meditation sessions, each time my mind was drifting away with thinking I went back and focused on the voice of the meditation guide which helped me take the focus away from my thinking and back onto the meditation session. I used guided meditation for about a year. Then, once my meditation skills grew stronger, meaning I was able to more easily and quickly quiet my mind, I switched from guided meditation to other techniques which I will share with you later in the book.

In a meditation session, when we are able to stop thinking we give room for other voices to enter our consciousness that otherwise would be obstructed by the noise of our mind. Meditation helps us hear messages of inspiration, guidance, warning, and support from our Team members, from other spirits, and from our Higher Self, or soul. Of course meditation is not the only way or the only time that we can communicate with our Team. As discussed previously, when we do the necessary daily spiritual work we can receive messages throughout the day in all kinds of ways such as intuition, gut feelings, signs, or inner voice. However, during meditation when we *intentionally* take the time to connect and request a communication in a session setting, we can be more specific regarding what we need or want to talk about. Also, in a meditation session, concentrating on quieting the mind will also have an effect on the clarity of the communication with our Team members as opposed to connecting to them in the course of the day when there are naturally more interruptions and additional life noises. In life, when we are angry, worried, or stressed-out for example, we surround ourselves with heavy energy that affects our mental state. When we meditate, once our mind is quiet and we are able to ascend to a higher level of consciousness, we can purify and clarify that heavy energy which helps our negative emotions such as anger, frustration, stress, and even physical discomfort can melt away. Pay attention to how much better you feel after a meditation session regardless of the physical and mental state that you might have experienced prior to it. Use meditation to be with yourself. Especially these days when life is hectic, busy, and noisy. Spend some time with yourself and by yourself, even for a short period of time. You will greatly benefit in every way. In these kinds of meditation you can enjoy time alone away from others and away from the noises of life. Using meditation as a way to be with yourself will also help you to take this time to reflect on your life, to see what it is you need to do and what it is you need to change in order to improve yourself, as well as your life in general. Meditating by yourself can also help force you to count your blessings. The reason I use the word force is because, in life our blessings are most likely obstructed from our view by our Ego Entity who influences us to concentrate on what we do not have and have not achieved rather than focusing on what we do have and have done! Making it a habit to count your blessings each day will not only help you to become a more grateful human being, which is a spiritual attribute, but will also help you to look at the "cup of your life as half full" which is a much more positive attitude.

Over the years I have often heard the Archangel Michael explaining that we "Come to this planet alone and leave alone, meaning that although we have people that we love and care for and that need us as we need them, the life that we live is ours and no one else's". And so it is important that we put ourselves first, in a kind and spiritual way, of course. The Archangel Michael also explained that putting ourselves first without feeling guilty about it is not a selfish act, but rather a selfless one. For example, when a mom takes some time alone to meditate, even at the expense of spending less time with her children, not only will she benefit but all those around her, including her children, will benefit as well.

Using Meditation for Prayers

Meditation can also be used for prayers and, as a matter of fact, prayers are a form of meditation. When we take our time to meditate in order to pray, a few things happen to us all at once. First, once we concentrate on our prayers, we take the focus away from our thinking mind which keeps it quiet. With a quiet mind we can enjoy the great benefits of a successful meditation session such as the more effective communication with our Team. When we pray, we literately surround ourselves with the Creator's Light which affects our energy. It helps us to become more relaxed, serene, and often to cry with joy. The vibrational energy of prayers helps us to invoke additional Light Beings such as additional Archangels and Ascended Masters that will join our permanent Team and will increase the amount of "ears" that are listening to our prayers, which, of course, is always a good thing.

When I teach the concept of the Team, I come across people who get confused with who they are supposed to pray to, God or their Team members. As discussed earlier, the Creator, although very much involved and aware of our soul's progress and evolution, as well as our lives on Earth, is not involved in our day-to-day life, nor in our day-to-day prayers. Granting or not granting our prayers has nothing to do with how much he cares for or loves us. How can it, when he unconditionally loves all of us equally? And so our prayers' outcomes, although ultimately are being heard by God, has nothing to do with him. When we pray our requests are being heard and answered by the members of our permanent Team. Which means that our Team members are the ones who listen to our prayers and to what it is we want and need and then try to do all that is within their power to help manifest them. Sometimes, depending on the nature of the prayers, other Light Beings such as the Ascended Masters or other Archangels can help manifest our prayers as well. Having said that, it does not mean that now that you know God is not involved in granting your prayers directly that you shouldn't bother praying to him. On the contrary, including the Creator in your daily prayers by praising him and by holding gratitude for his love strengthens your *connection* to him. It is important to understand, however, that manifesting prayers, for you or for someone else, has many conditions, such as what is best for our highest good, divine timing, our incarnation's blueprint, and our soul's current overall growth and evolution.

In your daily meditation prayers you can obviously pray for yourself, for your life, and for your loved ones; however it is important to also include planet Earth, all of humanity, nature, animals, as well as the Creator, of course! When you pray for yourself you can pray for help in overcoming your Ego Entity's influence or assistance disciplining any negative weaknesses that are standing in the way of your spiritual growth. For example, if you are an angry person you can pray to become more calm and serene, if you are judgmental you pray to become more accepting. When you pray concerning your life it is, of course, perfectly okay to pray for external things that you want, such as more money, a better job, a bigger home, or a life partner. Praying for your loved ones can include their well-being and happiness, their security and safety, their future, and even to have a strong connection between you. When you pray for planet Earth, pray to Gaia, our mother Earth, and her helpers, the Elementals, to help nature and the animals as they, too, struggle to survive. Pray that our human race that also struggles at the moment will side with the collective energy of our souls and not with our collective Ego Entities, and pray to the Archangels, who love us so much, to help inspire us to be able to succeed at this. Pray for the poor, the sick, and, of course, no matter what, always pray for peace not war.

> **In a deep meditative state we can "leave" this planet and enjoy the magical feeling of no mind, no body, and no time! It is the closest we can get to the feeling of when we are back at home in the Spirit World.**

Meditation Tips and Tricks

In this section I will provide you with some important tips, tricks, and rules that you can use in your meditation sessions. I hope that this information, in addition to the general information about meditation I have provided you in the previous chapter, will help put you in the right direction to establishing a consistent meditation routine and strong and effective meditation sessions.

When we fully and authentically understand the importance of meditation for our spiritual growth, the connection to our Team, and our well-being in general, we will be able to more easily put meditation in priority the same way that we do with any other important and essential activity such as going to work, exercise, eating healthy, drinking water, spending time with your spouse and kids, cleaning the house, etc. However, once we are ready to start the practice we need to watch for the endless excuses that are influenced by our Ego Entity. Excuses that stand in the way of a successful consistent routine. Here are some of those excuses that I often hear from people and, in the past, even from myself. "Meditation frustrates me"... "Nothing is happening"... "My mind is way too busy and so I know I will never be able to shut it off"... "I don't know how to do it"... "I am not sure what's supposed to happen"... "I am already spiritual and don't need to meditate"... "I am already meditating throughout the day like when I drive, tend to my garden, do the dishes, write my book"... and the most common excuse of all is "I honestly have no time"!

Due to our Ego Entity's lazy and negative nature, planning a solid meditation routine is one thing, and actually sticking to it is another. This is why you must work very hard to ignore it and follow up on your plan to succeed. When it comes to meditation and your Ego Entity, you must once again stick to the concept of doing the complete opposite of what it wants you to do. For example, when you are ready to get up in the morning and meditate and your Ego Entity is trying to influence you to stay in bed because "It's not a big deal to skip it today... and I'll do it tomorrow". Just don't! Get up and meditate anyway.

151

In my work, I often hear important questions from people regarding meditation. I want to share them with you because I know their answers will be important and helpful to you.

How many times a week should you meditate?

Because the essence of meditation is the ability to quiet the mind from thinking, which is a very difficult task for us to achieve, meditation requires a great amount of consistency, dedication, patience, and most of all *practice*. With practice you will get better and more effective with your ability to quiet your mind and raise your energy to a higher level of consciousness. I recommend meditating six days a week, with one day off, at least until you feel that you can quiet your mind in a fairly short period of time. If meditating six days a week is not possible for you, then you will need to meditate four times a week, at the minimum, so that your practice can stay consistent. Less than that will not be very effective. The bottom line is, meditating only once or twice a week or every other week and expecting effective sessions is like expecting to be in shape without having regular and continuous exercise. You must practice it often and consistently. Also, from a common sense point of view, since meditation has many great benefits the more you practice it, the greater the rewards you will receive. Your connection and communication with your Team will strengthen, you will be able to align with your soul, you will feel better in your body and in your mind, and, of course, you will grow spiritually.

What is the Best Time to Meditate?

Over the years I have tried to meditate at different times throughout the day and I have found that a *morning* meditation is most productive. Morning meditations are also the preference of our Team in spirit. First, in the morning the mind tends to be less active than in the evening when the day's activities and interactions are there to think, analyze, or worry about. Second, in the morning we are obviously better rested and more refreshed (assuming that the soul was able to exit the body and recharge itself in the Spirit World). And thirdly, in the evenings, by the time we get home from work, tend to the kids, cook dinner, or finish chores for the next day, we can get busy and tired which makes it more difficult to find the time and energy to meditate. I know that there are people who meditate late at night after everyone is finally in bed which is of course great if that works for you. There are always exceptions to the rule; however, these people often find that a few minutes into their meditation they fall asleep. This is, of course, not a super effective way of practicing meditation. I am also sure that some of you who read this will claim that although morning meditations are most effective, their mornings are as busy as their evenings, or even busier. I recognize this because it is exactly what I used to tell my Team each time they try to encourage me to meditate in the morning. I also remember their answer when I tried to get their sympathy with this excuse. They said, "We understand; however, *if you just get up before everyone else does, you will find the time*". And so I did. For the last fifteen years, while Clayton and all our pet-kids are still asleep, I get up, I exercise, and then I go outside and meditate.

How long should a meditation session be?

There are not specific rules for how long a meditation session needs to be. I know that different techniques call for different lengths of time for a session, however, simply use common sense and keep the spiritual concept of balance as your guidance for how long you should meditate. In general, a five-minute meditation session is obviously way too short while an hour and a half session is probably too long. The reason sessions that are too long are not effective is not only because we usually don't have that kind of time to spend each morning or evening, but also because the longer the session the more likely the mind will sneak back in and start thinking again which, ultimately, will extinguish the productivity of the session. I find that a twenty to thirty minute daily session is sufficient unless you choose to add addition time for a specific channeling, healing, extra prayers, or just to spend a longer time relaxing with yourself.

I meditate every day. Why don't I feel, hear, or see anything?

As I have said many times, spiritual work in general and meditation in particular requires hard work, practice, and patience. This means that it will take you a long time to discipline, ignore, and defeat your Ego Entity, reverse the well-being of your physical and mental state to become healthy and balanced, and align yourself with the wisdom and power of your soul. It will also take some time to begin to realize all the great benefits that meditation will provide. First and foremost for any of you who claim that they do not see any results from their meditation sessions, I will tell you to remain patient and to not give up. I ask that you continue to be dedicated to the process and to practice. Then, I reassure you that one day, in the same way that it happened to me, things will change. You will start to sense things, internally and externally. First, you will most likely see your Team members as orbs and other different shapes of colored energies. As time passes by, and as a result of your dedicated practice, you will even be able to hear and see your Team members as well as other spirits and Light Beings. *And once again let me remind you, that if I did it, you can too!*

Signs of a successful meditation

Over the years as I continued to meditate, I realized that there were a few distinguishing signs that indicated to me that I was able to successfully quiet my mind and ascend to a higher level of awareness. The following are a few of these signs.

A No-Thinking Mind

When you are able to achieve a successful meditation session you will notice that your mind is no longer busy with its usual thinking. Although you might still have some thoughts that will breeze through your consciousness in the course of the session, they will be light in energy and short in duration. This means that you will be able to easily ignore them and continue on with your meditation. The kind of light thoughts that will still visit us in a meditation session will also be completely different than the usual heavy thoughts that we experience throughout the day. Thoughts that nag at us in an obsessive kind of way and that seem to be in control of us, rather than us being in control of them.

Feeling at Ease

Achieving a successful meditation will also help you to feel at ease. At ease with all the people that you share your life with, the ones that you get along with and the ones that you do not. That easy feeling will also help you detach from all the challenges, drama, or conflicts that you are experiencing in your life and gain a different perspective on them. The perspective of your soul. That spiritual detachment will also give you a deep sense that everything in your life is where it should be and will be resolved, sooner or later, and in the best way possible. In general, that easy feeling is a "no worries man" kind of a feeling.

Deep Sense of Joy

This is an undeniable sign. Once the mind is quiet and your energy vibrates at a higher frequency, you will experience the joy of your soul. This joyful feeling will immediately bring tears to your eyes and give you a sense of gratefulness. For your life, other people, your Team, the world, and the Creator. This kind of joy is a feeling that we are usually unable to experience when the mind is active and busy because the mind itself is an obstacle to the joyful feelings of our soul. Of course this does not mean that the only time we truly feel happy is while meditating. In life, I refer to the feeling that we have when we buy a new car, get a promotion, or lose weight as *happiness*, not joy. The happiness that we experience from things, people, material possessions, as well as achievements, are, of course, great and welcome but are insignificant in comparison to that incredible feeling of deep joy that we feel in meditation when we experience the joy of our soul.

Heightened Awareness and Stillness

In a successful meditation you will experience heightened awareness and stillness which will help ground you to the present moment where you can feel relaxed, serene, alert, and focused. When you are still and grounded in the present moment you are aligned with your soul and strongly connected to your Team. A heightened awareness will help sharpened all your senses. You will be able to hear more noises and sounds, both man-made and natural, that are further away and that you would not usually be able to hear outside the meditation session. You will also be able to more easily sense your physical body's energy field and the Chi within it as a tingling sensation.

Freedom from Time

During our life on Earth, time is a major contributor to our stress level, anxiety, and worries. Through successful meditation you can enjoy the wonderful and peaceful freedom of "no-time". In this timeless feeling your past will not haunt you and the future will not worry you. Because in the no-time dimension, which is where you rise to in a meditation session, all concepts of time merge into one and become the timeless moment of your meditation session.

Goosebumps and Tears

In your meditation sessions, and in general for that matter, pay attention to goosebumps because they are the reaction of your physical body to the touch of your Team members and other spirits. Tears, joyful tears that is, are the reaction of your physical body to their presence and to your soul. And so in your meditation sessions, experiencing tears of joy is a validation that you were able to ascend to a higher level of awareness and that your energy vibrated at the same frequencies as that of your Team. Tears of joy are also a validating sign that you are aligned with the energy of your higher self. In a meditation session when you experience goosebumps, enjoy the wonderful fact that your Team members and most likely other Light Beings such as Angels and ascended masters are hugging your physical body.

Chapter tip: follow the tips!

How to Quiet the Mind

The ability to quiet the mind from thinking is an important spiritual task that requires practice, dedication, consistency, and, of course, patience. In this section I will teach you how to do it. The rest of the work is, of course, up to you to do.

So far, I have explained that in a meditation session, in order to effectively communicate with your Team members you must first quiet your mind. If the mind remains "noisy", you will not be able to because your thoughts, usually negative and dramatic in nature, produce heavy energy that clouds up, and depending on how heavy the thoughts are, even blocks the communication channel that extends from the crown chakra at the top of our head and connects us to our Team. With a partially clouded channel, a person might still be able to communicate with their Team members; however the messages that they receive can get mixed up with their own mind's activities and make the communication confusing and unclear, to say the least. A completely blocked channel prevents any sort of communication to a person's Team members altogether. However, once you are able to quiet the mind, your Team members will recognize that the channel has cleared up which allows you to become more receptive to their messages and the communication with them can begin.

In a meditation session, becoming free of thinking can benefit us in other ways in addition to establishing communication with our Team.

The following are some of those benefits.

1. When we do not think, and the channel is clear and open, we can align ourselves with our Higher Self, our soul, and enjoy its wonderful, joyful nature, wisdom, and spiritual power.
2. When we are free of thinking we enter a state of awareness that helps us *detach* from our life's challenges and difficulties. With this detachment we can feel less angry, fearful, or frustrated, and be more neutral and serene which helps us to accept the challenges and difficulties, as well as our life in general, the way it is.
3. A quiet mind helps us focus our attention on the present moment which is otherwise completely clouded by our thoughts that are mainly concentrated on the past and future. When we silence these and become one with the present moment, we feel serene and are able to experience the magnificent feeling of "no time".

4. When our mind is quiet, even for a short period of time, we can take a well-needed mental break from the absolutely exhausting and draining feelings that our mind inflicts on us on a daily basis with its constant negative heavy thinking.

Before getting into the specific techniques that will help you quiet your mind, there is a basic principal that you must understand first. Our mind is limited in its ability to focus and this can be used as a technique. The mind can not think and listen intensely at the same time. Neither can it think and intensely smell, or think and intensely feel or sense all at the same time. And so when we intensely use other senses through various stimulation, *we take the focus, or attention, away from our thinking and thus quiet our mind.* Another effective way that can be used to help you quiet the mind is by intensely focusing the attention on your *breathing.* Observing your breathing as well as the way you feel when air comes in and out of your body will not only take your focus away from your active mind but will also help you practice one of the most important spiritual concepts that can benefit you in many other ways. The first and foremost is to help you relax. The reason I keep using the word "intensely" is because in order to take the focus away from your thinking, which is a difficult thing to do, only an *intense focus* on something else will do the job. Otherwise, if you try to lightly focus on the other senses, the mind, which has great power, will once again take control and immediately take over and continue with its usual annoying habit of thinking. Also, notice that I did not use *sight* as one of the senses that can be used in this technique. This is because seeing does NOT stop our mind from thinking. As a matter of fact, when we use our eyesight we can think even more because the more we see, the more we have things to think about, which is why it is best to meditate with the eyes closed so that we do not add any additional "food for thought" to our already busy mind. When you consistently practice the various techniques that help you take the focus away from your thinking and onto other senses, you slowly but surely take the power away from your mind because each time you do it you break the destructive habit of the mind's constant thinking. Also the more you practice, the faster you will be able to quiet your mind and keep it quiet for a longer period of time. Then, one day you will notice that YOU are the one that is in full control of your thinking and not your thinking having full control of you. You will be able to shut off your mind any time you wish, both during your meditation sessions as well as throughout the day, which is one of the most important spiritual tasks that we need to accomplish.

Reading and mentally understanding the principle that you can quiet your mind when you intently focus on other senses is not enough. You must practice the technique so that you can experience it for yourself, that when you focus on listening, hearing, feeling, or smelling, you WILL be able to stop thinking. Mind you, in the beginning your mind will be quiet for only a short period of time, perhaps for only a few seconds, nonetheless, the thinking will stop. However, the more you improve your ability to take the focus away from your thinking, your mind will remain quiet for a longer period of time and when you really master the techniques it will remain quiet for as long as you want it to.

The Various Techniques

In the beginning of my spiritual path, each time I tried to meditate, I had a very difficult time quieting my mind. It seemed that my mind was always thinking, noisy, and busy. Later, knowing the importance of meditation for my spiritual path and the connection to my Team and other spirits, I decided to commit myself to the process until I overcame the challenges of my overly-active mind. Over the years, I have tried many different meditation techniques to help me quiet my mind and effectively meditate. Next I will be sharing with you the different ways that I find most effective and fairly easy to practice.

When you read the information you need to try these techniques and find out which ones work best for you. Once again, remember that since we are all different, a certain meditation technique that might work for you might not work for another person or vice versa. Also, whatever technique you use, you must always give it a good try, not just for one week or even one month but longer so that time and practice will help you determine which ones work for you. In addition to the different techniques, I will also provide you with some helpful information, advice, and a few examples to help you better understand the way the different techniques work. I would also like to add here that you can use the various signs that I wrote about in the meditation chapter to help you determined how effective you are in your ability to quiet your mind and how successful your meditation sessions are.

Guided Meditation

I find guided meditation to be very helpful and effective. In my work as a spiritual teacher I advise people to practice guided meditation if they are new to their meditation path, on days when their mind is overly active, or if they simply want to change their current meditation technique. Guided meditation was also the first technique that I used to help quiet my mind at the beginning of my spiritual path. In my guided meditations, when I listened intensely to the voice of the instructor I was able to come back to the session, even when my mind was drifting off to thinking again. Also, using guided meditation forced me to follow some of the meditation instructions such as visualizing the light, interacting with animals, visualizing Angels and so forth, which literally guided the focus away from my thinking and back onto what I was supposed to visualize. Through guided meditation I also started to enjoy the fantastic feeling of a meditative state which helped me remain serene and feel less frustrated and more excited about my progress. Thanks to my guided meditation I remember feeling that my meditation sessions were finally going somewhere. The bottom line is that by using guided meditation as a tool, it helped me to quiet my mind and build a strong foundation for more effective meditation sessions.

There are different types of guided meditations that you can choose from and I will provide you with a few tips that will help you decide which one is best for you to use. First of all, you need to choose a guided meditation that you know will keep you interested. If you get a guided meditation that bores you, your mind will grab the opportunity to take control and interrupt with thinking again. For example, because of my great love for animals and nature the guided meditations that I usually used included any kind of nature elements. These include listening to the sound of the ocean, walking on a sandy beach, or visualizing a thick green forest. Other guided meditations had interactions with different animals, such as swimming with dolphins, riding horses, or walking in a meadow alongside various creatures like unicorns. My other favorite guided meditations that I used included Angels of any kind, in whatever settings, because of my great interest in and love for them. Also, when you are choosing a guided meditation, try to choose one that has specific instructions that are somewhat spiritual. For example, choose one in which you are instructed to visualize the Chi energy, the Spirit World, or interact with spirit animals, your Spirit Guides, or Angels. In general, a guided meditation that has a lot of spiritual things to do, so to speak, is very effective not only because it helps you better quiet your mind, but it also helps anchor you to the present moment and helps you rise to a higher level of consciousness. As for how long your guided meditation should be, you once again need to stick to the concept of balance. If you choose a guided meditation that is too long, for example, more than an hour, you risk the chance that your inpatient mind will interrupt the process since most people can not keep their mind quiet for that long. This is especially true for beginners. A long guided meditation session might also be overwhelming for you if you don't have much time to spare due to a busy schedule, especially if you are planning to practice meditation every day, which should be your goal. On the other hand, too short of a guided meditation is not effective either because it does take some time to go back and forth from thinking to intensely focusing. Besides, if you rush your guided meditation session, you will most likely miss out on a lot of other benefits that meditation has to offer once the mind is quiet, such as enjoying time by yourself and with yourself, relaxation, aligning with your soul, and, of course, communicating with your Team members. Ideally then, it is best to get a guided meditation that is not too long or too short, perhaps one that is about thirty minutes long, or dividing a long guided meditation into two separate sessions. The main point is to get one that enables you to remain focused on the meditation instructions for as long as you are able to keep the focus away from your thinking. In the beginning, on days that you realize your mind is stubbornly active and makes it impossible for you to effectively meditate, the session is essentially over. Wrap it up and try again the next day.

The Music/Sound Technique

Another effective technique that can also help you take the focus away from your thinking is by intensely listening to the sound of music. Listening to music in general is considered a spiritual practice because certain sounds produce a higher vibrational energy that helps us to ascend to a higher level of awareness, lifts up our mood, and improves our mental state. Since music is an uplifting, soothing, and fun activity, it is compatible with the uplifting, soothing, and fun nature of our soul. This is why a lot of different cultures and various spiritual practices use music as a way of expressing their soul's joy, praying, and connecting to spirits and the Creator. The music/sound technique has one main important rule that you need to follow when you practice it. Because different types of music produce different levels of vibrational energy, you need to try to choose more spiritual music that will resonate with your soul's energy. Examples of this type of music or sounds include flute, classical music, chanting, or drums. What you want to avoid is any sort of music or songs that are too loud, obnoxious, have, profanity, unkind or negative gestures, as this type of music produces a more heavy vibrational energy due to their negative and unspiritual nature. Also, choosing the wrong kind of music for this technique will go against what you are trying to achieve because you will end up taking the focus away from your heavy negative thinking and into a heavy, negative music which will not quiet your mind but rather bombard it even more. When it comes to choosing the right music you need to rely on your spiritual knowledge, intuition, and plain common sense.

The Intense Listening Technique

Another effective technique that can help you quiet your mind is by intensely listening to any outside noises, man-made or natural, in order to once again take the focus away from your thinking and onto your hearing. This specific technique is a little more difficult to practice than the previous ones especially if you are new to meditation and to the ability to quiet the mind in general. The reason for that is because in this technique you are on your own, so to speak, meaning that you do not have the help of a guided meditation instruction or music to help take your focus away from your thinking, but rather it is you who needs to constantly use your intense listening each time your mind is back thinking again. This technique is very effective in helping you achieve a quiet mind but does need a great amount of daily practice. Because this technique is based on intensely listening to any external sounds or noises, if possible it is best to practice it outside especially in nature where there are plenty of different sounds and stimulations that you can focus on. Although an outdoor meditation is preferable to an in-home meditation, it is by no means necessary (which, of course, is helpful to people that must meditate indoors). When you live in a city and meditate at home you can also use this technique even if you think that the house is completely quiet, such as early in the morning or late at night. This is because when you intensely listen to the sounds of the world you will realize that there are always plenty of noises and sounds that you can still intensely focus on instead of your thinking. When you live in the city you will obviously have more man-made noises to focus on such as a garbage truck or bus yet these noises can also be used to effectively quiet your mind. The bottom line here is that although sounds of nature might be a bit more pleasant and easy to focus on, other sounds or noises will also do the trick.

The intense listening technique is my favorite because I use the sounds of nature to help keep my mind inactive and quiet. For me, this technique is not only effective but also very special as it gives me the feeling that I am one with nature that I so love. I remember when I started this meditation technique, I could not believe how many different noises and sounds I was able to hear, sounds and noises that I had not even known were there, such as unusual birds and other animals that I had never even noticed. Now, in my morning meditations the different sounds that I hear resemble a jungle rather than a private garden. Also, over the years, the more I use this specific meditation technique, the sharper my sense of hearing has become. Now, I can even hear our neighbor's pond and water sprinkler system running in their backyard, five acres away from ours. Over the years, using this technique made me realize how many different sounds we miss when we continue to focus our attention on our thinking instead of on the beautiful sounds of the world and nature. As a matter of fact, how many things do we miss in general when we are consumed with our busy mind?

Feeling the Body's Energy Field

In this effective technique, instead of intensely focusing your attention on your hearing sense, you intensely focus on the body's energy field, meaning the Chi energy that is flowing within your physical body.

This specific technique is a bit more difficult for me to write about because other than describing what you are supposed to feel and how you are supposed to feel it, it is the kind of thing that, again you must experience for yourself. In order to successfully practice this technique, you first need to prepare yourself for a meditative state by closing your eyes and entering a serene state of mind. Intensely focus your attention on your inner body. Starting with the palms of your hands, rub them together for ten seconds or so to intensify the Chi energy and then try to sense the energy at the tips of your fingers as a tingly sensation. It is important to start with your hands first because it is the easiest way to get familiar with the way the Chi energy feels. This familiarity is important because once you know how it feels you will know what you are trying to feel. If you are new to this technique it is a good idea to first focus on the body's extremities, such as the hands or feet and then as you get better at feeling the inner-body energy you can move on to other parts or areas of your body, such as your back, shoulders, face, legs, chest, abdomen, and so forth. Once you are able to feel the tingly sensation of the Chi energy do not take your focus away from it. Continue to FEEL, and the more you feel, the less chance you will have that your mind will sneak in and take over. When you continue to intensely focus your attention on the Chi energy in your body, you will strengthen the intensity of that tingly sensation, making it easier for you to hold on to it in order to quiet your mind. Once you become good at this technique, you will be able to use it to quiet your mind instantly, anywhere, and anytime. In your meditation sessions, when you want to communicate with your Team, or anytime you want to take a much needed break from your active mind.

Daytime Activities Technique

Any of the previous techniques can be used in order to achieve a successful meditation session and strong communication with your Team members. The daytime activities technique refers to any daily repetitive activities such as driving, reading, cleaning, or exercising. You can intensely focus on the activity so that you distract your active thinking and quiet your mind.

Here are some examples of how this technique can be used.

You are washing the dishes after dinner and obsessively thinking about the confrontation you had with a close friend, your mind goes on and on repeating the incident and adding countless scenarios about what you could have said or done, what you need to do and how you need to act next time. In order to quiet the mind, you can use the activity of washing the dishes to help take the focus away from your obsessive thinking by intensely focusing your attention on the way the water feels on your hands and skin or on how the soap smells. Then, remain alert and on guard. Each time you realize that you are thinking once again, immediately go back to focusing on the other senses. I am not saying that once you are done washing the dishes, you will not think about what happened anymore. Unfortunately you probably will. However, by quieting your mind, even for that short period of time, you give yourself a mental break from the heavy thinking which can then lighten up your anger or attitude and help you look at the incident from a more positive perspective. Additionally, having been able to quiet the mind, even just for the length of the activity, meant that you won the battle with your mind, a great achievement in itself.

You can also use other daytime techniques and apply them to the same example. Let's say that, while you are driving, you are obsessively thinking about a fight you had with a friend. You can intensely focus your attention on your inner body's energy field. Or, if you are exercising, intensely focus your attention on your breathing. If you are mowing the lawn, you can intensely focus your attention on the smell of the fresh cut grass.

The daytime-activities techniques have additional benefits as well.

First, since the ability to quiet the mind requires a lot of practice, using the daytime techniques provides you the opportunity to continue to improve your ability to stop your thinking throughout the day.

Secondly, in the course of the day when you use the daytime techniques you immediately become energetically lighter and more spiritually open which then helps you recognize any messages from your Team members through various signs, your intuitive system, gut feelings, or inner voice. Messages that you will most likely miss when your mind is too busy thinking.

Thirdly, when you quiet your mind, especially during the day when you are overwhelmed with worry, stress, or fearful thoughts, you gain some peace of mind that will helps you regain your sanity from your negative mind's activities.

And fourthly, the daytime activities techniques are also very beneficial for people who suffer from panic or anxiety attacks. Because panic and anxiety attacks are the reaction of the body to the illusionary fear that the mind inflicts on it, when a person takes the focus away from these fearful thoughts and on to other senses, they help stop the attack.

Below are a few examples that will help you understand how you, too, can use the daytime techniques to help you overcome the unpleasant phenomenon of panic or anxiety attacks.

I have a client who used to suffer from severe panic attacks, especially each time he entered the elevator in the building where he worked. Then he practiced the intense listening technique. He described to me that the moment he entered the elevator he intensely focused on the elevator's music instead of on his thinking or on his anticipation of a panic attack. That diversion of attention did not gave his mind the opportunity to create any fearful thoughts and, as a result, he suffered no further attacks.

Another client who also suffered from anxiety attacks each time she drove over a bridge or over a raised highway interchange practiced the breathing technique. She described to me that once she was getting close to a bridge or a high interchange she immediately started to slow down her breathing and intensely focus her attention on the way she inhaled and exhaled the air. She also carefully guarded her mind and if it started to think again she immediately ignored it by once again focusing on her breath. This lovely woman is not afraid of bridges or of high interchanges anymore. As a matter of fact, she expressed to me that she actually enjoys the view once she drives high above all the other cars. With the help of the daytime techniques these two people won their battles against their fearful mind and became free of their panic and anxiety attacks.

In summary, the ability to quiet the mind requires hard work. With each specific technique you need to be extra patient with yourself, especially at the beginning when you find it difficult to hold your focus on something other than your thinking. However, once you are able to stop thinking, you will improve your life in many ways as well as carve a path for effective and clear direct communication with your Team members which I will discuss in the next few chapters.

> **If you do not make the effort to quiet your mind from its endless amount of useless, noisy, and unnecessary thoughts, you become energetically heavy creating an incompatibility with the light energy of your soul and your Team members, which is obviously not a very good thing.**

CHAPTER EIGHT

The Power Of Visualization

Visualization is a powerful spiritual technique that will improve your life in many ways including helping to strengthen your connection with your Team members. Visualization also has many other benefits which I will cover later in this section.

Once you are able to connect and communicate with your Team members, seeing them through visualization will make your relationship so much more personal. In general, visualization can be used any time of the day; however, it is most effective when it is being used in a meditation session once your mind is quiet and you are able to reach a meditative state. Some people are better at visualization than others but, with enough patience and practice, everyone can successfully use this technique and enjoy its powerful benefits. I will describe in detail the main ways in which you can use and effectively practice visualization.

Connecting to your Team Members

When you visualize your Team members you make your relationship with them more personal, and therefore stronger. It is very important that you visualize your Team each time you meditate and, if possible, throughout the day as well. As discussed earlier, how you visualize your Team members does not matter, what matters is that you believe that they are there and that you trust in the concept of visualization as a way of strengthening your connection to them.

To visualize your Team members you need to meditate. Close your eyes and quiet your mind using any technique that can effectively help you do that. Then, with your "spiritual eyes" visualize your Spirit Guides, Guardian Angels, Archangels, Nature Spirits, and any departed loved one that you sense or know is a part of your Team or that you simply wish to call on. When visualizing your Spirit Guides and Guardian Angels it is important that you try to have as vivid and detailed visions as you possibly can. For example, do your Spirit Guides have a masculine or feminine energy? Are they male or female? Can you vividly visualize the clothes that they are wearing? How about their facial expression? When visualizing your Spirit Guides you can also use your intuition to help you determine how they prefer to appear. Perhaps as an American-Indian warrior, an artist, a monk, a gypsy, or a businessperson. Now what about your Guardian Angels. How do they look? Do they have wings? If so, what color? What shape? Do you have a male Guardian Angel or a female one, and so forth. When visualizing the four Archangels you can use my description of the way the Archangels look in the Archangels' chapter or you can visualize them yourself using the same technique above. When visualizing a departed loved one it is very important to avoid visualizing them from a time in their life on Earth when they were unhappy, ill, going through the dying transition, or in their hospital bed. Visualizing a departed loved one should always be from a time in their life when they were healthy,

171

content, and joyful. Here are few examples. When you want to contact a departed spouse or life partner, you can visualize him or her on your wedding day when you were both hopeful and joyful. If you lost a child you can visualize him or her at their high school graduation. A close friend can be remembered from a time when the two of you went on an unforgettable fun road trip together. And if you want to visualize your departed grandmother, picture her in the kitchen cooking your favorite food for you that she knew you loved. You get the idea.

Here are a few tips that you can use when visualizing your Team members.

If you are having a difficult time visualizing them, then create a look that is simple in details and easier to memorize. I also recommend using the internet to search for images of Spirit Guides, Angels, or Nature Spirits in order to allow your mind to take a snapshot of these images. Once an image is imprinted in your mind it will help you to start your visualization. If you do use an image from the internet, let's say of a Guardian Angel, try to add specific characteristics to the look that makes it unique since it is YOUR Guardian Angel. For example, perhaps you can visualize them with unusually shaped wings, a smile with dimples, unique facial expressions, and so forth. Just remember to be vivid and creative.

Once you are pleased with the way your Team members look through your visualization, which may take some time to achieve, stick to each of their specific looks and do not change them. That will make your visualization clearer more effective, easier to memorize, and most importantly, more personal.

Guard your doubtful mind! Our mind is uncomfortable and unfamiliar with many spiritual concepts. This is why ignoring it is crucial for the success of any spiritual practice in general, and visualization specifically. This means that once you have a clear vision of each member of your Team, do not think too much. Do not debate if the look you visualize is right or wrong. Trust that your Team members will love the appearance that you give them and, most likely, the vision that you will end up with is how they wish for you to see them anyway.

Using Visualization to Get What You Want

Through the power of visualization you can "give life" to anything that you intend to receive, accomplish, or create. The important rule that you need to follow when you use visualization to help you is that once you have visualized what you want, you must surrender the outcome to the magical power of your visualization and remain patient.

Here are some examples that will help you better understand this concept.

You have a job interview. On the morning of the interview you meditate and visualize yourself at the time of the interview relaxed, informed of the new position you wish to get hired for, and confident in your appearance and energy. You also visualize the person who conducts the interview to be spiritually open to your energy and receptive to what you have to say and intend to offer. Then you continue by visualizing the phone call or email that informs you that you got hired. You then seal this hopeful visualization with a vision of you feeling joyful and secure with this position for many years, creating prosperity and fulfillment.

You are planning to buy the house that you really love. You meditate and visualize your loan application going smoothly through the process and effortlessly being approved. Then you visualize yourself and your family quickly going through the moving process and then enjoying a joyful future together in your dream home.

You are going through a divorce. Through the power of visualization you can create what you wish for. An easy divorce process that is free of conflict and drama by visualizing you and your ex to-be remaining civil, kind, and loving to one another, as well as accepting of the divorce outcome. If there are children involved, you visualize them easily and smoothly going through the process with you and the transition to having two separate homes. You can also visualize you and your ex remaining friends so that any interaction or visitation with the children is peaceful and pleasant.

I work with a lot of couples who decide to end their marriage. Unfortunately, many of them are going through a very difficult time handling the divorce to a point where the stress, drama, and the despair of the process affects their well-being and the well-being of their children and other family members.

I want to briefly talk about divorce from the perspective of spirituality in order to give you another point of view that can help you if you are getting a divorce or know someone else who is.

Our ex-spouses or ex-life partners are most likely our soul mates with whom we had a soul contract. That contract of the relationship we had with them was planned prior to entering this life and had a great importance to our soul's overall growth and evolution. Fully and authentically accepting this spiritual fact will help you better understand that no matter how ugly, difficult, or nasty your relationship was, or the divorce process is, this human being with whom you shared your life had a crucial role in your incarnation because of all the potential growth experiences that the relationship has provided for the two of you. Also, if you happen to have other soul contracts involved in the plan, like children, then you both

174

have a crucial and significant role in their incarnation and their soul growth. Because of this spiritual fact, you need to try not to judge, be hateful, or unkind to your ex. And, no matter what, you must always wish him or her the best in their upcoming lives without you, pray for their well-being, love them, and thank their soul for its important role in your life on Earth. Of course spirituality does not mean stupidity. If your ex is unmanageable, unpleasant, cruel, or even dangerous, you must obviously stay away from him or her and protect yourself and your family in every way possible. However, even then, as a spiritual person, you will still need to love them, wish them well, and hold gratitude for their involvement in your life. Energetically speaking and from a distance, of course.

Visualization of Your Spiritual Growth

Through visualization you can create the spiritual person that you wish to become by "seeing" yourself as a kind, authentic, loving, Ego-less, and a soul-aligned human being. When you visualize how you want to be you give power to your intentions that then brings them to life. Of course, common sense says that your daily actions, decisions, and behaviors, in addition to practicing the necessary spiritual work that must be done on a daily basis, you need to support the visualization of that beautiful spiritual person that you aim to be because one does not happen without the other.

People sometimes ask me, if in addition to visualizing themselves as a spiritually aware human being, they can also visualize themselves having money and becoming rich. They are often nervous that visualizing themselves as being rich is not particularly spiritual. Well, the answer to that question is yes, of course you can visualize yourself as rich as you would like to be. Asking for money, whether it is by visualizing yourself becoming rich or by asking your Team members to help you get there, is perfectly okay. In fact, our Team members always try their best to help us achieve a secure and prosperous life. Once you have money, however, you must always guard yourself from allowing money to control you instead of you controlling your money. This means that you do not allow your money to influence you or your life in negative ways, such as by becoming arrogant, obnoxious, superior to others with less money than you, continuing to want more and more money even though you have plenty (which of course is a bottomless pit), or putting money itself and the earning of money as a priority in your life before your family, your well-being, or your spiritual growth. The bottom line is that asking for money, as well as having money, is perfectly okay. What you do with it, and how you behave once you have it, is what you need to observe.

Using Visualization for Energy Healing

In meditation, visualization can also be used for healing ourselves, other people, and animals. Before describing the way it can be done, it is very important to first understand a few spiritual rules about any energy healing. As discussed earlier, sometimes in an Earthly incarnation, illnesses, disorders, and even certain chronic symptoms, have a lot of different purposes that have to do with the soul's pre-designed plan and overall growth. And so receiving any kind of energy healing does not always deliver a cure. However, because energy healing helps the physical body to help itself, it will often offer some kind of relief physically, mentally, and emotionally. When it comes to how effective an energy healing treatment is, it has to do with a few different things such as the person's openness to the spiritual concept of energy healing in general, if the person is fearful or doubtful of energy healing, and the mental and emotional state of the person at the time of the treatment. The effectiveness of a treatment also depends on the ability of the practitioner as an energy healer, and his or her overall mental and physical well-being. This means that if their own energy is depleted and drained, or if they are in a stressful mental state, or even if they are angry at the time of the treatment and not centered and calm, the treatment will indeed be compromised and unsuccessful. It is also important for me to mention here that in order to use visualization for energy healing for either yourself or for other living beings, you do not need to be a "certified" energy healer such as a Reiki Master, for example. An effective meditation session, positive intentions, and strong visualization abilities, in addition to the powerful Chi energy, is sufficient to help yourself or someone else in need. Having said that, becoming a "certified" healer does add a few important spiritual benefits that can strengthen the intensity of the energy which can speed up the healing process. Finally, in addition to visualization, there is an abundance of good information to study the various ways in which energy healing can be used for healing. Once again, I recommend that you search for reliable and authentic sources of information that can help you be better informed about the beautiful concept of energy healing.

Self-Healing

You can use the self-healing visualization for any minor symptom or discomfort that you might experience such as a headache, backache, or cold, or a more serious illness such as a heart problem, pneumonia, or even cancer.

When you want to use visualization to heal yourself you need to first achieve an effective meditative state in which your mind is quiet, you are serene, and have anchored to the present moment. Then close your eyes and visualize the Chi energy, either in a white color or an emerald green color, the color of healing, wrapped around the specific area or organ in the body that is in need of healing. Then you stay very still and continue to visualize the area basking in the Chi energy. You will need to continue with your visualization for about fifteen minutes or so in order to allow the Chi energy, which has its own intelligence, to do its job and work on the problem.

Remember that while doing so your mind will get bored and try to take over the visualization process with thinking. As always, do not let it. If you realize that you are starting to think again, take the focus away from your mind and into the visualization of the Chi energy.

Many years ago when I started to use this technique on myself and had a hard time visualizing a certain organ in my body that I wanted to work on, I once again used the internet to search for a specific image that I needed in order for my brain to take a "snapshot" of it. For example, if I had a discomfort in my stomach, like an upset stomach, I would look up an image of the body's digestive system. Or if I had a headache, I would look up an image of the brain. Then, in my meditation session, I would find it much easier and more powerful to be able to visualize my stomach or my head being wrapped with the Chi energy and being healed. This technique of looking up images online can also be used for the visualization of colors. If you have difficult time visualizing a color, like emerald green, the color of the Chi energy, or any of the Archangels' signature colors, search the name of the color on the internet. Once you have a picture of it on your screen, stare at it for a few seconds so that your mind can take that snapshot for your memory. When you try to visualize it again I am sure you will find it helpful.

Self-healing visualization is a very effective and powerful technique that can help you feel better in a fairly short period of time. Even if it takes the Chi energy some time to affect you, or if your illness, disorder, or discomfort has a deeper spiritual meaning that the Chi energy is not meant to change, you will, nonetheless, benefit by feeling more relaxed, peaceful, and at ease.

Healing Others

In order to use visualization to help others, you basically use the exact same self-healing technique in which you visualize the Chi energy wrapped around the organ or the area in the body of the person that you are trying to help. When you are helping others, it is also a good idea to first call the person's name out loud and express your intention to help them with whatever it is that they need. For example, if you want to use visualization to help your child who has the flu, you call out your child's name and state that, through your visualization, you intend to help your child's body get rid of the flu and feel better again. In this example you can also continue to visualize your child happy and healthy again, playing on the swings with the other kids. Also, when using visualization to heal others, in order to strengthen the healing it is a good idea to visualize the person in your mind in addition to saying their name aloud assuming that you know who they are and what they look like. When I do distance energy healing for people or animals whom I have never seen, I request that they email me their photo, or photo of the animal so that I can visualize the Chi energy wrapped around them as well as their problem area or organ in their body.

I want to add a quick note about energy healing for animals and pets. Energy healing, of any sort, is very beneficial for all animals. Since animals do not have an Ego, and therefore do not experience doubt the way we do, when we work on them with energy healing they naturally remain energetically "open" for the Chi energy to enter their body and more effectively do its magic. Energy healing treatment for animals is very powerful and amazingly effective. An energy healing for animals is so powerful in fact, that the moment the treatment starts, the Chi energy immediately calms the animal down, relaxes it, and causes it to fall sound asleep. Over the years, I have witnessed energetic and vibrant puppies, and adult animals that were running excitedly prior to the energy treatment, once the Chi energy entered their body, immediately became calm and peaceful and fell asleep for the entire length of the treatment. If you, or someone you know, has a pet or an animal that is not well, not only physically but also emotionally or mentally, such as being too hyperactive, depressed, or has separation anxiety for example, use the above visualization healing technique to help them. As a Reiki Master and an animal lover, I am happy to say that over the years I have witnessed so many amazing and magical cases where the Chi energy helped cure many cases of sick and injured pets and animals.

Think about all the things that you want to have and to create in your life. Then, visualize those things happening to you in the exact scenarios that you wish for them to unfold. Then, remain patient and observe the magical powers of your visualization manifested exactly how you imagined!

CHAPTER NINE

Direct Communication

So far in the book I have spoken about the different ways in which we can indirectly communicate with our Team members, such as through our intuitive system, gut feelings, and signs, for example. However, there are other ways in which we can receive important information and messages of guidance, love, and support directly from each one of our Team members. I call this direct communication. Over the years, people have asked me how I started my direct communication with my Team members. In the next few sections I will describe the various ways in which I communicate with them. Before reading these chapters, however, I would like to remind you again, that in order to create a strong foundation for clear and direct communication, it is important that you use the information in the theory part of the book as well doing the necessary daily spiritual work in the practical part. If you try to shortcut the process by skipping any of the necessary steps prior to your direct communication, such as working on your mind-body-spirit, creating a dedicated meditation routine, or patiently practicing your ability to quiet your mind, you will not be able to directly channel your Team and understand their messages, no matter how desperate they are to reach you. For example, you can not possibly expect an effective direct communication, or an indirect one for that matter, if you engage in drama each day, allow your body to become unhealthy and unbalanced, remain overly stressed-out, engage in a five-minute meditation session once every other week, or allow your mind to engage in over thinking all the time.

Direct communication with our Team members, as well as other spirits, requires your ultimate faith and trust. Faith in the sense that you authentically know and believe with all of your heart that your Team members are real and are there by your side anxiously waiting to communicate with you, even more so than you are with them. Trust that with a persistent and dedicated practice routine, you will be able to achieve effective direct communication with any of your beloved Team members any time you wish to!

Inner Voice Communication

In life, one way in which we can directly communicate with our Team members is through our inner voice system. In this chapter I will describe for you how this can be done.

Inner voice communication with your Team, especially in the beginning, can be best achieved in a meditation session. However, later on you can also use it throughout the day, as well. Before you are ready to start your inner voice communication, it is very important to first achieve a strong meditative state where your mind is quiet, remains quiet for the whole length of the communication, and your channel is clear and open. First, you simply need to start talking to your Team and then just listen as intensely as you possibly can to their reply.

In the beginning it is best to use simple words and short sentences because a simple, non-complex dialogue in addition to a fairly short session will make it easier for you to hear and understand their messages while still being able to keep your mind quiet of thinking. Of course, as you improve your ability to hear and understand your Team members through your inner voice communication, as well as keeping your mind quiet for longer periods of time, you can raise the complexity of the communication and the length of the session. I also recommend that in all your communication with your Team, whether it is through inner voice or through any other technique, its always a good idea to include some expressions that have the word *love* in them. Using the word love in your communication with your Team members will strengthen your connection with them because the word love itself is a powerful energetic force that carries with it the positive collective energy of humanity, planet Earth, the spirit world, and the whole universe. Also, exchanging words of love between you and your Team, as well as between you and another person, or between your soul and other souls is something that provides great immense joy to everyone involved. After all who doesn't love to be loved?!

As for my own communication with my Team we always make sure that we express our love for one another in the beginning and at the end of our communication sessions, as well as throughout the day. We do this every day. There are also a few sentences that we often add to our words of love. My Team's frequently repeated sentences are, "We are right here", "You are never alone", "Do not be afraid", "Everything is okay", and "You are safe". And mine are, "Don't leave me", "Remain in my life", "Help me to be fearless", "Help me grow", and "Protect me."

Differentiating Between the Two Inner Voices

Inner voice communication can be confusing in the beginning because your Team channeling may sound the same to you as your own internal thinking or inner voice. This is the reason why most people's main concern about this form of communication is that they will not be able to tell the difference between their own inner voice and that of their Team which is, of course, a legitimate concern. However, this is an effective method of communication and once you invest the effort of practice, apply trust and faith in the process as well as in the outcome, you will reach a point where you will be able to easily recognize who communicates with whom, you with yourself or you with your Team.

Next, I have provided you with some helpful tips and powerful techniques that will help you to better recognize the difference between the two inner voices.

1. Using the Love Word

In the beginning of your inner voice communication, especially in your first few weeks or so, I recommend that you start the session by saying "I love you" and then intensely listen for your Team's reply which will most likely be "We love you too." The reason for this is because hearing an inner voice saying "I love you" will help you overcome your doubtful mind in regard to who is doing the communicating. This is because "I love you" is not something that we naturally tell ourselves. Meaning that when we hear an internal voice expressing that they love us it is certainly someone other than us.

2. Positive vs. Negative

Our inner voice is our internal mind activity that is not being expressed out loud. It is our inner voice dialogue and, due to the influence of our Ego Entity, is more often than not negative in nature. Unfortunately, even on days when the dialogue of our inner voice is positive or uplifting, as human beings that positive internal dialogue will often have some form of negativity attached to it such as fear, criticism, judgmental attitude, or anger. On the other hand, because the members of our Team are energetically pure and loving Light Beings, the essence of their communication through our inner voice can only be positive in energy and loving in nature, as they are incapable, technically speaking, of any negativity.

With enough time and practice you will be able to easily recognize when it is your Team members who are communicating with you and not your own inner voice's activity by the positive, loving, and negative-free nature of the messages and information that you are receiving. For example, let's say that through your inner voice communication with your Team, you believe that you channeled a fear- based message that caused you to become scared and uneasy. Well, think again, because you are wrong. This message was not and could not be a message from any of your Team members because that would be impossible. That message was not a message at all but rather a fearful inner dialogue that you had with yourself through your own inner voice. It is important to understand here that even though messages from our Team can not possibly be frightening or negative, they can indeed be strict and serious when they need to be, including important teaching, necessary warnings, as well as crucial information or premonitions that they know we must hear. Although these messages might be difficult for us to hear, they will never frighten us, make us feel uncomfortable or uneasy, and they will certainly not be negative. Because despite the tough nature of the messages, they will always be loving and positive in energy as they originate from your Team's immense love for you. There is a big difference between strict and frightening.

3. Different Energies

Another way in which you can differentiate between your own inner voice and that of your Team is by sensing the different energy that your Team's messages produce in contrast to your own internal thinking. Because our inner voice is a reflection of our mind's activity, often busy, obsessive, and negative in nature, the energy of these thoughts is dense and heavy which can negatively affect our mental state. On the other hand, our Team's communication is always positive, loving, and uplifting; it produces a softer and lighter energy that can affect our mental state in a positive way. Once again, the more you practice your inner voice communication the easier it will be for you to clearly and more effectively sense the different between these two distinctive energies which will then help you to immediately recognize your inner voice from your Team's messages.

4. Different Sound

The two inner voices, our own and that of our Team members, not only have a different energy and feel different, but they also sound different. I will try my best to explain the way they both sound so that you can better understand what I mean. Because our inner voice is *us*, it is coming from within us, or right up front so to speak. It sounds closer, stronger, and louder. On the other hand, our Team members' communication, although used by our inner voice system, is still coming from *outside of us* and sounds quieter, softer, and somewhat from a distance, in the background if you will. I know that this description might be confusing which is why in order to fully benefit from this tip you will need to apply the information to your practice so that you can experience the two subtly different voice sounds for yourself. This is a very helpful distinction that, once you are able to recognize it, will leave you with no doubt as to whose voice you are listening to.

5. Speaking and Listening

This technique can be used as a tool to help you become more familiar with the way your inner voice communication with your Team feels and sounds. You can also use it to communicate with your Team; however, due to the way this specific technique works, the messages that you will be receiving will be short. Here is how it works. When you are in a meditative state, you will need to say aloud any sequence of short words. For example, you can start counting, one, two, three, four... or you can say the alphabet. Then, at the same time that you are saying the words, you need to intensely listen to the background for any inner voice communication from your Team. The reason this technique is effective, is because you can not simultaneously speak out loud and engage in any internal dialogue with yourself. The speaking will leave your inner voice system available for your Team members to use to communicate with you.

In summary, regarding the different ways your own inner voice sounds as opposed to your Team's, stick to the core principal. If you hear any internal negativity of any kind, it is your own inner voice. All uplifting, positive, loving messages, regardless of the nature of the information, are from your Team members. Then, as with any other spiritual concept, it is very important that you discipline your doubtful mind and skeptical attitude and trust the information.

> **Inner voice communication requires a great deal of practice but the results are very much worth the effort. Once you are able to effectively do it, you can communicate with any of your Team members about anything and everything, at any time you wish. Now, how great is that?!**

Touch Communication

Our Team members can also communicate with us through touch. Touch communication has the same purpose as any other form of communication, direct or indirect. It is to get our attention for any messages, warnings, or information that they wish for us to know or see, to help us realize that they are nearby and are present in our lives, and of course to tell us that they love us. In the same way as any other communication, whether it is through intuition, signs, inner voice, or automatic writing, when you feel your Team touch communicate with you the first thing you need to do is acknowledge that you know it is them and express gratitude for their communication. Then, smile and enjoy the sensation. If your direct communication is fully developed, you can also ask which one of your Team members touched you and what the specific message is that they wish to express. If you are unable to get these answers you can either rely on your intuition of who it is, as well as for the reason of the communication, or you can always just enjoy the fact that your Team are nearby trying to get your attention through their touch.

Knowing how fearful humans beings can be, our Team members are very careful with the way they touch us so that we don't panic. Any kind of touch communication that we will feel from our Team is always well planned, gentle, pleasant, and just plain fantastic. Depending on the degree of a person's spiritual awareness, openness to spirit communication, and inclination to fearfulness, not all people will experience the same sensation when their Team touches them. Some might not even experience it at all.

Obviously, if a person is not open to the concept of the Team, or spirits in general, the person's Team members will not take the risk of touching the person knowing that the unusual or strange sensation that he or she will feel by some unseen force will be interpreted by the mind as a fearful or negative experience which will diminish the whole point of the communication. On the other hand, when we are more spiritually aware, are open to our Team's existence, and are able to experience some of the other methods of communication, feeling the sensation of touch communication is something that we can experience on a daily basis that can bring us great joy. In my case, when I was still new to spirituality and was not aware of my Team yet, they never tried to contact me through touch. Then, as years went by, and I became familiar with the beautiful spirits that were surrounding me and I sharpened my abilities to communicate with them, every once in a while I started to feel the sensation of their touch. Now, touch communication with any of my Team members is something that I experience several times a day and when I don't, I make sure I ask them for it.

Next, I will describe the different ways that our Team members communicate with us through touch. Remember though, that since we are all different in the way that we connect with them, the description of the sensations that we might feel when they touch us can be slightly different from one person to the next. Nevertheless, the general concept of how it is supposed to feel will be similar for all of us. Also, pay attention to the specific purpose of each specific communication. It will help you become more familiar with them and their different objectives when your Team will attempt to get your attention with touch communication.

Goosebumps

This touch communication can be used by all the members of our Team as well as other Light Beings. Goosebumps are often the reaction of our body to our Team's or spirits' touch. When any of our Team members touch any part of our body we will immediately feel the sensation of goosebumps especially on our arms, legs, neck, or scalp.

Third Eye Sensation

This form of touch communication is mainly used by our Spirit Guides. Our third eye, which refers to the invisible eye that can provide us with perception beyond ordinary sight, is located in the middle of the forehead, above and between our physical eyes. When our Spirit Guides touch us at our third eye location, we will feel a tingly pleasant sensation all over our forehead. Because this specific touch communication is commonly used by our guides it usually indicates that there is something in our life that we are missing and that we need to pay attention to or something that we need to be aware of. Other times, through touch communication by our Spirit Guides on our third eye, they are trying to inspire us to develop our third eye ability, use it to grow spiritually, better our life on Earth, and, of course, more easily communicate with them. So when you feel the sensation in that area, acknowledge your Spirits Guides. If you are already able to communicate with them you can ask them for the specific purpose of this communication or you can rely on your intuition to figure out what their message is. If all else fails, and you cannot determine the purpose of the third eye touch communication, you can simply enjoy the pleasant sensation and make sure that you hold gratitude for the fact that you made physical contact with your beloved teachers in the Spirit World. By the way, everyone can gain the ability to "open" their third eye. Try to look for reliable materials and helpful information that can instruct you how to do this. Then you can apply what you have learned to a consistent practice routine.

Top of the Head Sensation

This touch communication is mostly used by the Angel members of our Team. This includes our Guardian Angels, the four Archangels, and any other Angel that is around us at any given time. When the Angels use this specific touch communication they actually touch or stroke our hair on the top of our head as a way of expressing their affection and love for us which, of course, feels wonderful. This touch communication can either feel like a tingly sensation in that area or it can actually feel as if your hair were gently moving. Other than affection and an expression of love, the meanings of this specific communication are support and validation that Angels do exist and are around us.

Eskimo Kiss

Although this touch communication can be used by our Spirit Guides as well as our Guardian Angels, it is primarily used by the Archangels. The purpose of this communication is to express their love for us with an Eskimo kiss in the same way that we do it here on Earth. What I call the Eskimo kiss is when an Archangel kisses the tip of your nose, creating a pleasant itching or tingly sensation in that area that gives us the urge to scratch it. When I sense this specific touch communication, it is usually at the end of my meditation sessions when any one of the Archangels is telling me, "I love you and I'll see you tomorrow!". This is by far one of my favorite touch communication modalities because I love both the sensation as well as the message. Besides, who doesn't love to be kissed by an Angel?!

Pressure on the Cheeks

This touch communication is commonly used by one of our four Archangels, Michael, Gabriel, Raphael, and Uriel, one or more of whom always accompany us in life. The sensation that we experience when they touch our cheeks feels like a soft, light, and pleasant pressure. This is usually in the middle of the cheek on either the right or left side of our face. In order to recognize this specific touch communication it is best if you are in a meditative state or are very focused and alert. The specific side of the face that you feel the pressure on is very important because it can help you determine which Archangel is communicating with you through their touch. If you feel the pressure on your right cheek then it is the Archangel Michael or the Archangel Raphael that is initiating the communication. Pressure on your left cheek is the Archangel Gabriel or the Archangel Uriel. Of course, in order to further identify who specifically is initiating the communication you can use any other communication such as the inner voice, automatic writing, or rely on your intuitive guidance. If you are able to see the Archangels unique signature colors or are able to visualize them, then you will know which one of them is touching you. You can refer back to my description of their unique colors in the Archangels' chapter. The purpose of this specific touch communication depends on which Archangel is touching you. For example, if you feel the pressure or touch on your right cheek it is the Archangel Michael making his present known to you and telling you that he is helping you with your fears or it can be the Archangel Raphael reassuring you that he is helping you with your well-being. If the sensation is on your left cheek it is the Archangel Gabriel supporting you with extra strength or the Archangel Uriel giving you hope. Please notice that you can also ask any one of the four Archangels to touch your cheek, which of course, they are always more than happy to do. Or you can also ask a specific Archangel that you need most at that time to appear by your side and make their presence known to you by touching your cheek.

Ear Ringing

This touch communication is used by the Archangels and sometimes by our Guardian Angels as well. Ear ringing is very common and I often hear people report that they are able to experience it. I am sure that most of you, at one point or another in the course of your life, have also experienced a ringing sensation in your right or left ear and so I am hoping that you will understand what I mean when I use the phrase "ear ringing". Touch communication through ear ringing is mostly used by the Archangels. In the same way that you can determine which Archangel is initiating the communication in the cheek touch communication, the specific ear that is ringing can also help you narrow down which Archangel is trying to get your attention. The right ear is the Archangels Michael and Raphael. The left ear is the Archangels Gabriel and Uriel. Once again this touch communication can also be used by any other Angels that are with you at that time in addition to the permanent Angel members of your Team.

Light Touch on Face or Neck

This touch communication is commonly used by our departed loved ones, those who are a part of our Team, as well as any other people who have crossed over and were close to us in life. This kind of communication feels like a light, brief, pleasant touch on the top of the head, the forehead, or the neck. The purpose of this specific touch communication is for our loved ones in the Spirit World to communicate to us that they are by our side, love and support us, and most importantly, to let us know/reassure us that they survived their physical death. When you experience this type of touch communication and are unable to sense or determine who is trying to communicate with you, you can request help from the soul (which, of course, they will be more than happy to do). The way that they can help us determine who they are is by, once again, using our intuitive system, inner voice, (assuming we are familiar with that type of communication), as well as other signs, such as a familiar cigar, cigarette or perfume smell, that was unique to them. They will use signs that can help us to immediately know, without a doubt, who is communicating with us.

Tapping on Shoulders or Back

This touch communication is used mostly by our Guardian Angels. As mentioned earlier, when our Team members, especially our Guardian Angels, need to warn us or protect our life they will indeed intervene with any life-saving measures to communicate with us. One of these interventions includes this specific touch communication in which they will tap on our shoulders or upper back. The feeling of this tapping will be very obvious. Meaning that, if your Guardian Angels chooses to use it to warn you, it will feel as though an actual person behind you is tapping to get your attention. Because of its urgent nature, this specific touch communication is different in that it feels like a light touch or a slight pressure. Depending on the degree or severity of the message or warning this touch communication can feel like a strong physical contact by an invisible presence. And, as you can imagine, it might frighten some people, especially if they are not spiritually aware or open enough for this sort of spirit communication. Nonetheless, frightening or not, if our Guardian Angels realize that they must get our attention immediately they will indeed use the tapping touch as a part of their dedicated job of protecting and keeping us safe. It is also important to understand that when our Guardian Angels use this specific touch communication, it is not only to save us from getting hit by a car when we are ready to cross the street in an unsafe way, for example, but can also be used in order to help us reconsider any kind of a foolish, reckless, decision or action that can harm us or will affect our well-being in any negative way. Now that you know this, it is important to put it into practice. If you feel this kind of communication, immediately stop and consider its implications on your current decisions or actions. It will help guide you and can possibly save your life!

Tug on Clothing

This kind of touch communication is also used mainly by our Guardian Angels and essentially has the same purpose as the tapping on the shoulders or back touch communication. When they need to get our attention in an urgent way in order to save us from any external disasters or internal destruction our Guardian Angels will tug on our clothes, usually at the end of the sleeves or at the bottom of our shirt or sweater.

Tears of Joy

Experiencing tears of joy is not a touch communication per se, but rather our body's reaction to the powerful energy that is exchanged between our Team members and us when they use touch communication or when they are close by. When any of our Team members as well as other Light Beings, such as Angels or Ascended Masters, or any of our departed loved ones, communicate with us through touching, stroking, kissing, or hugging us, we can experience the deepest and most powerful feeling of joy. That powerful feeling of joy expresses itself in our physical body through tears. When we shed these tears of joy we not only share this love with spirits, but we also appreciate the present moment the way it is, feel grateful for our life, and all the people, without exception, that are in it. We can also feel a strong connection to our Team and to the Creator. That joyful feeling will also help us to recollect our true nature as souls. Experiencing tears of joy is a wonderful spiritual phenomenon. As I mentioned previously, feeling joy has nothing to do with any external happiness in our life on Earth. For example, when we buy a new car we might shed tears of happiness and excitement, but these tears are not the kind of tears that I am discussing here. The happiness tears that we will experience from our new car will feel shallow and be short-lived in comparison to the tears of joy that we shed from having our Team members touch us. Having said that, obviously there is nothing wrong with shedding tears of happiness for being proud and excited to have finally been able to buy a longed-for car, or to shedding tears for any sort of external success. It is merely to point out the difference between Earth-related tears of joy, which I refer to as happiness, and the "tears of joy" created by the Spirit World.

It is important to note that when it comes to touch communication, or any communication, direct or indirect, with our Team or other spirits, that the information I am providing you in this chapter as well as in the entire book refers *only* to any communication that you will have with your Team members or any other Light Beings. This means that once you are able to communicate with spirits you will need to be very wise and careful about whom you are trying to invoke, call on, connect to, or communicate with. If you are not careful you can and will attract a low vibrational, negative spirit or entity that can harm or influence you in a negative way. Let me explain what I mean. Over the years I have encountered people who have recklessly used improper methods to communicate with spirits such as Ouija boards, various voodoo practices, or certain dark witchcraft or magical practices which attract nasty and negative entities that scratch them, burn their skin, kick or slap them, affect their home or their family members, as well as influence their mind in a variety of negative and even dangerous ways. There is good spirit communication and there is bad spirit communication. You must handle any spirit communication you want to have cautiously, wisely, and most of all respectfully. Even though you have plenty of protection from your Team against any negative forces, if you make a conscious effort to invoke spirits in reckless ways, they will not be able to protect you from the consequences of your actions due to your free will.

In order to control who is communicating with you, stick with the light. Do the necessary daily spiritual work that will align you with your soul and keep you connected to your Team and to other pure

Light Beings. Stay away from irresponsible and reckless ways of invoking spirits that you have no business invoking so that you do not make it easy for anything that is negative in nature to enter your energy field.

Be good and attract good!

> **Being able to feel your Team members touching you is a great honor because you are actually able to connect your physical body with their ethereal one.**

Automatic Writing

Another way in which you can directly communicate with your Team members is through the ancient spiritual technique of automatic writing.

Automatic writing is a big name for a very simple, yet effective technique that helps you communicate with your Team and other spirits. Through automatic writing your Team members can communicate their messages to you, through your writing, by guiding your hand and pen. Automatic writing can be helpful to people who are having a difficult time using any of the other techniques to achieve direct communication with their Team, or they can use automatic writing as an additional method of communicating. In this section I will provide you with comprehensive information about automatic writing and, of course, how to effectively use it.

Automatic writing is similar to inner voice communication. With both techniques you will need to be very aware of who is doing the communication. Whether it is you with your Team members, or you with you. You will find that some of the rules, tips, and advice that

I have written about in the inner voice communication section will be similar to the ones in this chapter. For example, you can use the very same techniques to help you differentiate between your own inner voice and that of your Team. In automatic writing you can also discern between your Team's messages and your own writing by the content of the messages as well as by the way they feel and sound. This means that despite the nature of the messages or information, your Team's communication through automatic writing will always be optimistic, loving, positive, and light in energy. Whereas despite the nature of the content of your own writing, it will tend to be more pessimistic, negative, harsh, and heavier in energy. Once again, practice and experience will help you validate this information and discover for yourself how they differ from one another.

Over the years, I have heard from many people and have experienced myself, that when communicating with their Team members through automatic writing their handwriting as well as the type of words they use and the way the writing reads and appears is completely different from their normal writing. For example, when I channel messages in my automatic writing sessions, my English has better grammar than normal and looks and sounds more academic. Sometimes, depending on whom it is that I channel, it is even a bit poetic. My handwriting also becomes clearer and easier to read, understand, and has less spelling errors. Keep in mind that English is my second language, I have a heavy accent, and only completed a high school education. Therefore, when I see the writing at the end of an automatic writing session I am always amazed at the huge difference between my own writing and that of my Team members. Essentially, in an automatic writing session, although we are the ones who are holding the pen, we are certainly not the one who is actually doing the writing.

Important Automatic Writing Rules

First, in order to benefit from the automatic writing form of communication you must practice it often. Also, because the automatic writing process will usually not produce any effective results in the first few weeks and sometimes even months of practice, especially if you are new to any form of direct communication, you must discipline your impatient mind from unrealistic expectations of immediate results. Second, as with any other form of communication, direct or indirect, the spiritual work of your mind, body, and spirit must continue throughout the day, and every day, so that you can operate at a higher level of awareness. This will help you clear up your channel to your Team members and be more open to communication. Third, in an automatic writing session, a quiet mind is very important and has a direct influence on the degree of success of the communication. You must achieve an effective meditative state where the mind is completely "out of the way". Finally, you must work on your doubtful mind and negative thinking. You must trust in the concept as well as the process and have faith that your Team will help you succeed and directly communicate with them.

Automatic Writing Tips

1. For your automatic writing sessions I recommend that you buy a notebook that you will use only for your automatic writing. Try to purchase a notebook that looks and feels spiritual. This means, try to get one that not only looks nice but perhaps also has drawings or pictures of Angels or other pleasant Light Beings on its cover. Or, buy a notebook that has any other spiritual imagery such as meditation symbols, nature, and so forth. The point is to have a notebook that is special and unique for both you and for your Team.
2. Try to make sure that all of your automatic writing communication messages are in that one specific notebook

and not on scattered papers. Any messages from your automatic writing sessions are not only valuable because they contain important information for you, your life, or the lives of others, but they are also very precious because they are the fruit of your efforts to communicate with such wise, pure, Light Beings who care and love you so much; you certainly do not ever want to lose them.

3. Once you've got your special notebook, a pen in your hand, and are ready to start your automatic writing session, it is a good idea to write the day of the week and date at the top of each page in order to document the process as well as the results of how effective you are becoming in both receiving and understanding the communication from your Team through the writing. Additionally, some of the messages and the information that you will be receiving will be in sequence. This means that during the session your Team might communicate certain information that will need to be continued in the following session. So organizing the messages by documenting the days and dates of the sessions is very important.

4. The best time of the day for your automatic writing sessions is in the morning. Automatic writing is done while in a meditative state and essentially is a form of meditation. Like meditation, it is best done in the mornings when you are fresh and well-rested, as opposed to the evenings, when all the day's activities act as "food for thought" for your eager mind. With practice, you will become better at quieting your mind anytime you want to, even outside of your meditation sessions, and therefore the more flexible you can be in choosing a convenient time for your sessions, even evenings.

5. People ask me if they can use their computers for their automatic writing sessions. Well, I suppose they can. I never really liked it because I, and more importantly my Team,

as well as spirits in general, prefer to communicate the old-fashioned way, with a pen and a notebook! I also feel that although some of the twenty-first century technologies that we now have are great and helpful, communication with spirits through automatic writing is best done in the old-fashioned way, with a pen and paper. I must say though, that I have come across people who use their computer to do their automatic writing sessions and claim that they are quite successful at it. Therefore, I suppose it can be done. If you are one of these people that use the computer for your automatic writing sessions, there are two things you should keep in mind. First, despite your Team's preference for using a pen and a notebook, once they realize your preference for using the computer for the automatic writing communication, they will use your fingers and the computer's keyboard to get their messages across to you in the same way that they would have used your pen and a notebook. And secondly, make sure that you apply the information I am providing you in this section, the rules and tips, in addition to any other reliable information that you might want to gather about automatic writing in general, to each one of your sessions, whether you do them via the computer or with a pen and notebook.

The Practice

To begin your automatic writing session you need to enter a meditative state where your mind is quiet and your vibrational energy is high. Then, in the same way as with the inner voice communication, especially during your early attempts, you need to start with a simple, non-complex dialogue that includes some loving expressions. For example, you can start your session by addressing each one of your Team members by saying out loud while writing, "Greetings to you my beloved Spirit Guides, my Guardian Angels, the Archangel Michael, Archangel Gabriel, Archangel Raphael, Archangel Uriel, and any elementals that are with me today, I love you all". You can also address any specific departed loved one that you would like to add to the communication. Then you need to ask while writing, "Can you please communicate with me through my pen and notebook?" Then, while holding your pen *lightly* in your hand, you simply start writing, not thinking, just writing! As the session continues, try your best not to look or examine what you write. Just continue to write until you intuitively feel that your Team needs you to either pause the writing so you can reply to them, or end the session altogether. If you need or want to reply to your Team, it is always a good idea to express your excitement and gratitude for their messages in addition to whatever it is you want to tell them. Then, as always, never forget to thank them for communicating with you, and to seal the session with words of love.

In the course of the session, as you continue to write, you need to guard your mind to make sure it remains quiet. At any point that you realize that your mind is starting to wake up from its quiet mode and start thinking again, you need to immediately refocus on the writing or use any other technique that will help you to shut it off again. It is also important that, at the end of your automatic writing session, when you are ready to read the messages that you have channeled you must guard your mind from its usual judgmental and doubtful nature. Do not allow it to come up with any negative doubtful scenarios such as "It is more probable that I wrote that", "What if I am doing it all wrong?", "What if all of this is nonsense?" "It seems like I am wasting my time", and so forth. Once again, remain in control of your mind, and not vice versa.

Now I understand that it might sound as if there are a lot of things that you will need to do and remember all at once in the course of the session. In the beginning this is the case. But let me explain that an automatic writing session, especially in the beginning when you are new to this form of communication, is not something that you want to rush. It is very important that you take your time and establish a strong meditative state before the session even starts. During the course of the session you need to put a great deal of effort in continuing to keep your mind quiet of thinking as well as to control any doubtful or negative thoughts you might have about the process or your ability to succeed. Sometimes you might need to simply stay still until your Team recognizes that you are ready and open to write down their messages.

After your first attempt, regardless of the level of success that you achieve, you must continue to practice your automatic writing form of communication again the next day and then the next day after that. Consistency is the way that you will be able to improve your ability to clearly and effectively communicate with your Team members. As time goes by, and as you get more comfortable allowing your Team members to use your writing as a way to communicate with you, you can increase the complexity of the communication, as well as the length of the automatic writing sessions. You can use automatic writing to contact any member of your Team for advice, guidance, words of support, or any general information that you would like to have about your life, other people's lives, as well as any other information or spiritual knowledge that you wish to gather about our planet, the Spirit World, and the universe. You can also use automatic writing to get your Team's help and inspiration, especially your specialized guides who can help you with any project or work that you are doing, such as writing a book, an article, starting a blog, and so forth.

A final important note that you must keep in mind is that at the beginning, and at any other time in an automatic writing session when you feel that you are stuck in a way that, no matter what you do and how quiet your mind is, you are unable to receive any messages through the writing, you need to understand this is perfectly normal. As with any other spiritual practice, some days will be more difficult to succeed than others. When you encounter one of these days, wrap up the session and with fresh attitude of trust and faith, call on your Team members the following day and try again. The most important concept that you must keep in mind is the basic rule of thumb for any spiritual work that you do in life: giving up is not an option!

> **When you are able to let your Team "do the talking" through automatic writing, you improve your life, your well-being, your spiritual awareness, your connection with them, and your writing.**

CHAPTER TEN

Make It Personal: Name Your Team Members

In this chapter I will discuss the importance of addressing your Team members by their names as it relates to your connection with them. I will also teach you how to get the names of some of your Team members through direct communication. First, however, I want to talk about names in general. This is because they are important in our daily lives, as well as to our soul's Earthly incarnations and, of course, to our connection to our Team.

When we are in the Spirit World as souls we are all one. We are all connected to the source. Within the source, we do not need names to tell one from another. Nor do we need names to refer to one another when we communicate since all communication among souls/spirits is done in an energetic and direct consciousness-to-consciousness form. However, during our lives on Earth, because of our spiritual amnesia and insensitivity to energies, names are obviously important because it helps us recognize one another and helps us communicate with one another individually. A name also has a vibrational energy that makes the connection between individuals more personal.

Here are few examples.

Pay attention to how distanced and disconnected you feel when you happen to talk to a stranger on the street without knowing their name. Then, feel the shift in energy when all of a sudden there is an exchange of names between the two of you, the energy will become softer, you will smile more, the conversation might even get more intimate, and you might even gain a new friend. Also, when you meet a person that you have not seen for a long time and suddenly remember his or her name, pay attention to how pleased they become when they realize that you actually cared enough to remember them by their name. As for myself, I always try my best to remember the names of people who cross my path. If I happen to forget someone's name, I politely admit that I, regretfully, forgot their name and ask them kindly to remind me. It makes me happy to see how pleased they are that I care. Then of course, I try my best to not forget it again. In life, using names in a conversation is very helpful. When you converse with another person whether it is at work, in your personal relationships, or with someone you just met, try to use their name often when you communicate with them. It will make both them and you more comfortable, happy, and at ease. It will also strengthen the connection that you have with them, energetically speaking. With a stronger connection they will focus more on what it is you are trying to discuss with them. Using a person's name is also particularly helpful when you have an important conversation with someone close to you such as your spouse or your child. It is also helpful during a conflict, assuming you lower the level of drama first, and use a kind tone of voice when you mention their name. In a conflict, softly using the other person's name will also change the vibrational energy in the room from heavy to light which will then "clear the air" for a more positive outcome. Try it out. Practice on your husband, wife, children, parents, or relatives. It works!

The name that we are born with is also very important because it was our soul who chose it. Prior to entering life on Earth, an important detail that our soul carefully includes in the incarnation's blueprint is the name that we are going to be given when we are born. Although it appears as though the parents choose their children's names, it is in fact the newborn baby's soul, in addition to the soul of the parents that makes certain a specific pre-designed name will be used. The reason our name is so important as far as our soul is concerned, is because the combination of the letters that comprise our name, in addition to the time of birth (our astrological map) has a direct influence on any potential growth as well as the incarnation's overall plan.

Our Team Members' Names

On Earth, when we communicate with our Team members it is important that we address them by name so that we can energetically strengthen our connection with them and make the relationship more intimate and personal. It is the same effect as when we interact with other people in our life and use their names.

The Angels' Names

Angels do not have names. They were created as powerful and wise energy Light Beings. As discussed earlier, they do, however, have their own unique vibrational energy, their own unique color, their specific purpose, but they do not have names, per se. The names of the four Archangels, Michael, Gabriel, Raphael, and Uriel, were not given to them by God when they were created. Their names, as well as the names of other Archangels, are names that we, human beings, gave them during the centuries of the existence of humanity on this planet. Of course, the Archangels love their names very much and are very proud of their names because we human beings, a species whom they love so immensely, invented them and use these names to call on them.

Our Guardian Angels do not have names either. They, however, like to express their own preference for the specific name that they would like us to address them by. For example, when I started my direct communication with my two Guardian Angels, my female Guardian Angel told me that she really like the name "Iris" as she always thought it was a lovely name. My male Guardian Angel asked me to refer to him by a name that he likes, "Judah". Since that time, some fifteen years ago, I respectfully address my beloved Guardian Angels by their chosen names, Iris and Judah.

Our Spirit Guides' Names

Our Spirit Guides do have names and so we need to make the effort to learn them. The names that our Spirit Guides chose for themselves are names that they picked from a specific incarnation on Earth that they considered to be a great success. Not an external success of course, but a success that has to do with the amount of spiritual growth that their soul was able to accumulate in that life as well as the amount of contribution that was made to the collective energy of humanity. Our Spirit Guides often choose a name that represents a lifetime that they were proud of when they were here on this planet. A common problem with the names of some of our Spirit Guides, however, is that sometimes these names are very ancient, unfamiliar, unusual, and different from any name that we might be familiar with and it often presents me with a challenge when I try to channel these names in readings. Over the years, however, I have also channeled plenty of Spirit Guides' names that were easier to understand because they sounded more familiar to me, such as Peter, Duncan, Sam, and Isabel to name a few.

The Elementals' Names

In their dimension of the nature kingdom, the Elementals also communicate with one another in an energetic and telepathic way and do not require personal names when they interact. When they communicate with us here on Earth, the elementals do not necessarily like us to give them a specific personal name. They prefer that we either refer to them by Elemental, Nature Spirit, and sometimes even Angels of Nature. Equally acceptable to them is when we use the more generic names that we human beings gave them, such as fairies, gnomes, pixies, and so forth.

Our Departed Loved Ones' Names

As souls, our departed loved ones no longer have names. They dropped their name at the same time that they "shed off" their body and mind. This occurred when the incarnation came to its end at the time of death. However, when you wish to communicate or call on any of your loved ones in spirit, you will need to call on them by the name that they mostly used in their life on Earth which is not necessarily their birth name.

Here are a couple of examples.

If you lost someone that on Earth did not use his or her birth name because for whatever reason they changed it at some point in their life, then you should use the new name that they changed it to when calling on them. If you lost a friend that on Earth went by a nickname, one that you alone referred to him/her by or one that everyone called them, it is best If you use that nickname rather than the given name when you wish to call on that departed friend's soul. The point here is to use a name that the person used to love the most and identified with the most up until the time when they crossed over. Using the name that they went by will not only make the soul joyful but will also strengthen the connection between the two of you by making it more intimate and personal despite the fact that you now reside in two different dimensions. Also, when you wish to call on the soul of your mom, dad, or any of your grandparents, it is always better to call them by their relation to you and not by their name. Meaning that your mom's soul would prefer it if you called her mom or mama rather than her name and your grandfather would very much love it when you call him grandfather or grandpa or any other loving nickname that you used to refer to him by on Earth.

Channeling Your Team Members' Names

Before describing the way you can channel your Team members' names, there is an important point that you need to keep in mind. When it comes to the process of getting your Team members names, stay light and playful and do not take it too seriously. While trying to channel your Spirit Guides' and Guardian Angels' preferred names is important, you should not be concerned if you got it right, wrong, or even if you did not get it at all. Our Team members do not care if we channel their names correctly nor do they care what names we end up using for them. All they want is that we get a name, stick to it, and then address them by that name to create a more personal and more intimate relationship.

In order to channel your Team members' names it is best to use the automatic writing technique so that your Team members can use your pen and paper to spell out their name for you. You can also use the inner voice communication technique; however, if any member of your Team has an usual name that is difficult to understand or hear, you may have a hard time channeling it.

As always, before starting your automatic writing communication, you will need to enter a meditative state in which your mind is quiet of thinking and your vibrational energy is high. Then, call on your

Guardian Angel first. Visualize him or her standing in front of you, slightly to your left. Take your notebook and your pen and ask them for the name that they prefer you to use. Then, write it down. Once again, do not doubt the process or worry if you received the name correctly. Don't try to change it to another name after you wrote it down in the notebook because it will most likely be a new name produced by your mind and not your Guardian Angel. Just trust in the process and stick with the name you received. Believe and trust that the name you wrote down is the exact name that your Guardian Angel wants you to use. Next, call on your Spirit Guides and see them standing in front of you, slightly to the right. Repeat the exact same process using the automatic writing technique to get the name of your primary Spirit Guide as well as of your trainee Spirit Guide if you are aware of, and/or are able to communicate with them.

If you are unable to get the names of some of your Team members due to a series of ineffective automatic writing sessions then you need to come up with names for your Spirit Guides and Guardian Angels on your own. You can do it several different ways. First, you can come up with a name that feels right to you, intuitively speaking, because as you can recall, our intuitive system is commonly used by our Team for communication. And so when a name all of the sudden appears "out of nowhere" in your consciousness, grab it, and use it from then on. Or, if you happen to know how your Spirit Guides look for example, meaning if they are male or female, if they look like a monk or a gypsy, be creative by giving them a name that is appropriate for the way they appear. You can do the same process, if you are able to, by visualizing your Guardian Angel. Or, you can be playful with the names. For example, I have a client who could not channel his Guardian Angel's name. However, because he is a pilot and senses that each time he flies his plane his male Guardian Angel is by his side protecting him, he named him "Sky". His Guardian Angel told me that he loves it! Another client named his Spirit Guide "Ocean" because he is a professional sailor and because of his great love for the sea. Another woman called her Spirit Guide "Frank" because she said that when she visualizes him he looks like the singer Frank Sinatra. So once again, when it comes to naming your Team members, it is important to stay light, be playful and creative, and always respectful.

Once you have identified names for each member of your Team, make sure that you memorize them and use these names on a daily basis. Obviously, you need to use the names of your Team members when you wish to communicate with them and because it will strengthen your connection with your Team in general. It is also a good idea, to call on them by name "out of the blue", at any time throughout the day. If for no other reason but to simply express your love for them and your gratitude for their involvement in your life.

> **Our Team members are our teachers, protectors, and eternal friends. When we refer to them by name their involvement in our lives as our teachers, protectors, and eternal friends becomes much more personal and intimate.**

SUMMARY

When I committed to writing this book my aim was to teach you, the reader, the core spiritual concepts and practical application of these concepts in order for you to further the spiritual growth of your soul during this incarnation. During the writing of this book, I had several ultimate goals to share with you that I would like to highlight and recap in this final chapter. It is my hope that by truly learning and applying these core concepts, you will be able to start your spiritual path or continue even further down the spiritual path you are already on.

First, it is my hope that by sharing with you the process that I used to get to know my own Team, and the way I have been able to connect to and communicate with them you, too, can use this information to do the same with your own Team members. It is also my hope that once you establish a relationship with your eternal friends and teachers in spirit, you will know without a doubt, and especially during the times that you might feel lonely, that you are never, ever, alone in this world! Second, I believe that the information I have provided you with throughout this book about the other spiritual subtopics will help you grow in spiritual awareness as well as to view your life from the perspective of your soul and not from the perspective of your mind. I know that this fundamental change will improve your life in so many surprising and dramatic ways.

Finally, I hope that after reading my book, you will feel positively uplifted and excited about this Earthly life of yours and that you will be empowered with the knowledge that you now have. Primarily, that YOU have a major role and a meaningful purpose, with a direct effect on your soul's growth and evolution, on your fellow human beings, on this planet, and on all of God's creation.

I also wanted to highlight some of the most important guidelines that I hope will help you in your future spiritual work.

1. *Trust and Authentically Believe*

Fully trust and authentically believe in the spiritual concepts behind this book's information. Otherwise, if you "half-believe", you will not benefit from any of the advice, teaching, or techniques, no matter how hard you try. For example, if you do not authentically believe in the concepts of signs because you keep telling yourself "It's probably just a coincidence", each time you get one from the members of your Team, you will never be able to fully enjoy this way of communication with them. Or, half-believing in the existence of Angels, will obviously negatively affect your connection with them as well as your ability to communicate with them.

2. *Dedication, Practice, and Patience!*

Spirituality, in all its forms, does not come easy for us human beings here on Earth. This is due to the spiritual amnesia that we have at the time of birth, the spiritually lazy nature of our species, the major obstacles that we can have from our physical and mental bodies, and, of course, our negative and destructive Ego Entity. So remember that connecting to your Team members, as well as working on your spiritual growth and awareness, always requires a great deal of dedication, practice, and of course, patience.

3. *Mute Your Ego Entity and Give Your Soul a Voice*

Remember, that by choosing positive actions and decisions that are compatible with the energy of your soul, and not negative decisions and actions that are compatible with the negativity of your Ego entity, you will then become aligned with your Higher Self, allow it to govern your life, and spread its wisdom and spiritual power out into this world.

4. *Value and Respect Your Life and Make Each Day Count*

Remember that your soul, with the help of your Spirit Guides, invested a great deal of time and effort planning your life for the sake of its overall growth and evolution and it counts on you to wisely and effectively use that plan for growth. Do not let your Ego Entity influence you to decide, act, behave, or interact, in unwise, foolish, or reckless ways that might jeopardize the success of this plan or worse yet, cut it short.

5. *Your Daily Mind-Body-Spirit Work*

Have a pact with yourself that from now on, until the day that you leave this planet, you must work every day on all the aspects of your self. Disciplining your negative mind, your Ego Entity, and balancing your physical, emotional, and mental body and using your soul to govern over your life. Remember, that ignoring any one of these aspects will shake up your plan to contact and communicate with your Team members and delay or even block you efforts at spiritual growth.

6. *Always and Forever Keep the Creator in Mind*

Keep in mind that when you make the effort to spiritually grow and better your life, you make God, that amazing force who created you, proud. Because when you positively change yourself, you also help to positively change others as well as the planet, which are all an inseparable part of his overall creation. How can that not make our Creator proud of you?

Dear Reader, I wish you all the best of luck with your connection to your beloved Team and with any future pursuit of spiritual growth. I wish you a fantastic, long, and joyful life, full of positive and fun memories that you can take with you to the Spirit World after this incarnation completes its purpose. Thank you all for joining me on this journey!

ABOUT THE AUTHOR

Miki Jacobs is an internationally renowned medium and spiritual teacher. Miki teaches people to communicate with their "Team" in spirit and view life from their soul's perspective. She also connects people with their departed loved ones. Miki and her husband rescue horses and other critters on their ranch in California.

CPSIA information can be obtained at www.ICGtesting.com
Printed in the USA
BVOW04s2135171114

375462BV00003B/11/P